MEMELOOSE
The Island of the Dead

BY E. F. WINTERS

Look for:
THE JOLIE CHRONICLES
Book One: SHARKS AND MINNOWS
Book Two: GHOSTS IN THE GRAVEYARD

Watch for:
THE KEEPERS OF THE TRUTHS
Book One: EBULON

EDITED BY J. L. WINTERS

MEMELOOSE
The Island of the Dead

E.F. WINTERS

Kenspeckle
Productions, LLC

MEMELOOSE is a work of fiction. Names, characters, places, and incidents either are the product of the author's imagination or are used fictitiously. Any resemblance to actual persons, living or dead, events or locales, is entirely coincidental.

2013 Kenspeckle Production, LLC

Copyright © 2013 by E.F.Winters
All rights reserved.

Published in the United States by
Kenspeckle Productions, LLC
Distributed by Lightning Source
for Print on Demand and as an e-book

Library of Congress Cataloging-in-Publications Data
E.F.Winters & Kenspeckle Productions, LLC
ISBN 978-1-940531-02-1

Printed in the United States of America

Book design by E.F.Winters & J.L.Winters

CHAPTER ONE

Tarak placed the edge of his bare foot onto the soft mat of pine needles, rolling the sole flat until it rested gently on the forest floor. Above him, pine trees stretched into the sky like long fingers. A blue jay cawed. A squirrel chittered. Summer held the forest close like an old man wrapped in his blanket for an afternoon nap. Silently, Tarak shifted his weight and stepped forward.

"Slowly, Ghost. Slowly," he whispered to the white dog at his side, keeping his eyes on the clearing ahead.

It was late summer in the high valleys beneath Wai-i-ka, the great White Mountain. The Moon of Drying Berries was at an end and Tarak's family would soon be gathering with his mother's people to celebrate Pi-ki-owish; the ceremony that re-made the world each year. There would be dancing and feasts.

It was a good time for a first hunt; a good time for a boy to become a man.

As slowly as if his arm were a tree limb moving in the summer breeze, Tarak drew an arrow from the quiver on his back. The wood of his bow felt smooth and familiar in his hand. Together

CHAPTER 1

he and the bow had added many small animals and birds to his mother's cook basket. But squirrels and pheasants were not important. A deer was all that mattered. Only a deer made a boy into a man.

The doe in the clearing ahead turned sideways as she grazed. Beneath the shadowed stripes of her ribs, Tarak could see the pulse of her heart beating. Did hers seem as loud to her ears as his did? His heart beat like the men's drums in the Sweat House.

This is it, Tarak thought, aiming for the dark line between two ribs. *The arrowhead must strike flesh.* A glancing blow off the rib would crush his hopes of leaving childhood behind today.

His friend, Ghost, twitched at his side, holding his strong body as tight as Tarak held his bow's string, waiting for Tarak's signal. The dog glanced up at his friend and made a soft, questioning huff. Still, Tarak did not move.

A line of sweat trickled down his leg, snaking around the back of his knee.

Now. It must be now, Tarak thought.

Movement on the far side of the clearing drew the attention of both boy and dog. Tarak squinted to see past the sun-flooded clearing to the shadows beneath the trees on the other side. Something moved.

A deep, low, rattle rumbled in Ghost's throat and he inched closer to Tarak, skin and fur touching. He would protect his boy, no matter what the threat. For wherever you found one, you always found the other: dog and boy, boy and dog; inseparable since the night Tarak's father first set the furry lump of a pup in his young son's arms.

Tarak had never been farther from home than the Salmon River but he knew the Takelma people from the North and the Eukshikni from the Big Lake, who sometimes visited the Kama'twa village. These strangers did not look like either of those people. Long, white, rabbit fur capes covered their bone-thin bodies. Their dry, brown skin looked like old leather. Their loin cloths were rags and their faces had been carved by a mean life and hardship.

Tarak had heard the village elders whisper about raids in the high mountain valleys. During the woka harvest, tribesmen from the east had attacked the Eukshikni and Maklak villages, taking food, hides, women and children. The elders said the raiders had killed anyone who stood in their way. They had called these men "the Snake".

Silently, the strangers spread out beneath the trees like blood spreading over the ground, heading for Tarak's doe. Ghost growled again.

"Hush, old bear." Tarak stepped back behind a pine tree, lowering his bow. His throat was tight and hot tears welled in his eyes. He leaned back against the tree, a battle raging inside him. He wanted to run out and shout at the strangers, *"Go away. This is my deer. Go back to your own lands. You don't belong here."* But he knew he could not. He had seen their faces. Words

CHAPTER 1

would not make these men go away. Their purpose was much darker.

Tarak shut his eyes and bit his lip. There would be no triumphant return for him; no feast, no celebration of manhood.

Someone must warn the village.

As if stabbed by the boy's disappointment, the doe raised her head and leapt for cover.

Ghost lunged forward, ready for the chase.

"No, Ghost." Tarak held him back, dropping to his knees and digging his fingers deep into his friend's thick, white coat. The sharp gasp of an arrow sliced the air. There was a dull thud and the doe fell.

Bitterness sat like rotten fish in Tarak's belly. He buried his face in Ghost's fur, breathing in the scent of sun-warmed dust, wood-smoke and pine; the smells of home and family. Tarak tucked away his disappointment and stood.

"Come, Ghost."

As the strangers cut open the doe's chest, digging into the cavity of its body to pull out the life-rich heart, Ghost and Tarak silently slipped away through the forest.

CHAPTER TWO

Tarak's feet pounded the trail, his dark hair flying out behind him like a crow's tail, Ghost keeping pace beside him.

He smelled the village before he saw it, the weathered plank roofs blending into the trees. But you could not mask the scent of pinewood smoke and acorn soup.

He skidded to a stop before his father. Ata', and his friends were gathered beside the family lodge.

"Strangers!" He gulped for air. "On the hilltop, Ata'. In the clearing." He pointed back up the trail. The men's hands grabbed their weapons as Tarak's mother came out of the lodge, his baby sister tucked into the crook of her arm. His other little sister followed, toddling along in her mother's shadow.

Ata' turned to his son. "Eukshikni? Takelma?"

"No," Tarak shook his head, his eyes wide. The men turned and started up the path. Tarak moved to join them. His father blocked his way.

"Not you. You stay here and look after your mother and little sisters," Ata' commanded.

CHAPTER 2

Tarak's mother, A'ni, removed her basket hat. Her dark hair, parted in the middle and fastened at each side with hemp string, shone like the hard, black rocks that hunters used to make arrowheads. Worry lengthened her round face.

"But you need me," Tarak protested. "I know where they are. I can show you the way."

"No." Ata' was unmoved.

"I am not a child, father." Tarak clenched his fists.

"You are not a man yet, either," Ata' said firmly. "You will stay." Ata' hurried to catch up with the others.

Hanging his head to hide the shameful tears that stung his eyes, Tarak peered resentfully through the curtain of his dark hair.

"It's not fair." He ground his toe into the dirt. "I am not a child."

Ghost made a huff that was not quite a bark and pushed his wet nose into Tarak's hand. Tarak looked down at his friend. "The doe was mine; mine for my feast. I had her. If it weren't for these strangers, there would be a feast tonight in my honor and I would be a man. Then they would not have left us behind." Ghost huffed again, smiling his doggy smile. Tarak ruffled the dog's fur. "We will hunt again tomorrow," he promised softly. It was hard to stay angry with Ghost around.

"Thank you for keeping my boy safe, old bear." A'ni patted the dog's head. His easy, generous nature had made him a favorite in the village.

"Keeping me safe? I think it was more the other way around, Mother." Tarak thrust out his chest. "Ghost would have run after the Snake and tried to bite them if I had not pulled him back."

"Then it is indeed lucky that you were together so you could look after each other," A'ni agreed, her dark eyes twinkling. "Anyway, you're home safe and that is what matters. Now put the fire out and make no smoke then take the message about these strangers to the other families so they do the same. Go now, quickly, and keep Ghost quiet. We do not want to draw any attention."

The baby's plump fingers grasped at A'ni's dentalia shell necklace. It had been a wedding gift from Ata'; the many shells telling everyone how much he valued her as his wife.

"This little one will have to marry well." Ani's smile stretched the three lines tattooed across her chin. "See how she reaches for wealth?"

"She will not be old enough to marry for many re-makings of the world." Tarak scowled. It was his future his mother should be thinking about. He was the one who was grown up now, not his little sister.

"Your a'cmu and Kari-wa are by the river," A'ni added as she took her older daughter's hand and led her to the lodge. "Tell them there is food to share in our cook pot then come straight back. You will sleep in the family lodge tonight."

CHAPTER 2

Tarak wanted to argue. He was old enough now to sleep in the Sweat House with the older boys and the unmarried men, but the look on his mother's face checked his tongue. Mothers could be very nice but by the time you were thirteen, you knew there were times you should not cross them.

With one last glance back up the forest path, Tarak and Ghost headed downhill into the village.

That night the children did not play games by the river and there were no stories by the campfire. The village went to bed in silence, lying hushed in the darkness, listening for the movement of shadows and praying for the safe return of their men.

The moon was high when Tarak's father finally climbed down the ladder into the lodge.

"They have gone." Ata' answered his wife's silent question as he leaned his bow and quiver against the plank wall.

"Was it the Snake?" Fear colored A'ni's voice.

Ata' nodded. "They've gone now. We tracked them traveling east back around Wai-i-ka. Still, we should be careful. Keep Tarak close for a few days. No hunting."

No hunting. The words crushed Tarak's chest like a weight. If he'd had a few more moments..., if he had shot the doe..., if the Snake had only not come so near his village today, they would be feasting him. Instead, nothing had changed. Feeling terribly sorry for himself, Tarak wriggled closer to Ghost's furry back. The old dog raised his head, looking back at his friend then let it flop back down, letting out a big, wheezy, sigh. Taking comfort in his friend's warmth and measured breathing, Tarak finally fell asleep.

CHAPTER THREE

Just thinking about going to Iri'waw's cave made Tarak's stomach squirm like a nest of worms. The cave was not like the comfortable lodges of the villagers. Kama'twa homes were built with their floors sunk down into the ground and had fur hides to sit or sleep on, baskets to hold things in and a welcoming cook-fire in the center of the lodge. Iri'waw's cave was an open gash in the face of the cliff that defined the valley, cut out long ago by the river. Damp and smelly, the cave was packed with herbs and talismans of power.

In a villager's home, each family's sacred items were kept, in a storage basket or leather parfleche in the place of honor just opposite the door, so everyone knew where they were and it was easy to be respectful and avoid touching them. Iri'waw had the skins of sixty animals in her small cave; deer, wolf, coyote, silver fox, fisher, and otter. Lengths of sinew strung with tails, wings, and feather topknots hung overhead or trailed down the walls. You couldn't even move without bumping into something that it was rude to touch.

Tarak had been to the cave three times since his Spirit Quest in The Moon of Falling Snow, but he didn't like it any more now than he had the first time. Being brave on a hunt was one thing. That was glorious, grown up and manly. But talking to spirits was something else altogether. Still, a boy's Spirit Quest was an important step toward becoming a man and it had to be done; scary or not.

Powerful spirits lived on the mountain. No one, except Iri'waw, climbed higher than the tree line--not even for Spirit Quest. The Elders told of a time long ago when the Old Man of the Mountain became angry with people and threw hot stones at them, chasing them from the mountain's slopes. Tarak's people pointed to the fields of stones ringing Wai-i-ka as proof of the story's truth. Sometimes they even saw smoke rising from the top of the mountain, coming from the old man's teepee.

When Tarak and the other boys came down from their time on the mountain, the others told stories about their visions or shared the new calling song they had been given to call fish, animals, or birds to help them, but Tarak's vision had not been like the others.

"Tell me what you saw up on the mountain, Tarak," Iri'waw had asked when it was his turn.

Tarak's mouth felt as dry as summer dust. Shame hunched his shoulders and fear squeezed his heart. What could he say? He had failed. He bit his lip.

"What did you see?" Iri'waw asked again, leaning forward and squinting to see him clearly.

CHAPTER 3

Tarak did not want to say it out loud but he could not lie to the old woman.

"Nothing," he said, his voice barely a whisper.

Iri'waw sat back and sent the other boys away. When it was only the two of them, she asked again.

"Tell me, Tarak, what did you see?"

"I saw nothing."

"Nothing?" The old woman raised her eyebrows. "The world looks as it always does? No four legged, no flyer, no creepy crawly came to speak to you? No axe'ki?"

"No." Tarak shook his head. "Everything was gone." The nothing had been more frightening than any axe'ki demon he had imagined he could meet.

"Explain this to me." Iri'waw's voice was quiet and even. Tarak thought she would be angry or disappointed, but she did not seem to be either. He licked his dry lips.

"I don't know. I was sitting there, waiting, looking around and then I must have fallen asleep because when I looked around again there was nothing but darkness."

"It was night?"

Tarak hesitated. "Maybe. I don't know. But it must have been, right?"

"I don't know. I was not there. This is your vision. There was nothing else there in this darkness but you? Nothing at all?"

Tarak swallowed hard, remembering. No matter how wide he had opened his eyes, no light had come to them but he had not been alone. Something, or someone, had been there in the dark. He remembered eyes staring at him; dead eyes, and more. His stomach flipped and bile rose in his throat.

"There were bones...many bones all over the floor and piled in the corners. It was a place of death."

"So there was a floor and corners. The floor and corners of what, Tarak?" Iri'waw prodded him gently. "There are no corners in 'nothing'. There is no floor. Only a place would have these things. You were somewhere, Tarak. The question is where?"

"Don't you know? You must tell me Iri'waw."

The old woman shook her head. "You must remember."

Tarak hung his head, feeling hot and weak. "It makes me feel sick to think about it."

Iri'waw pressed her lips together. "I am sorry but you must try. Could you hear anything; the wind, trees, leaves rustling...anything?" Tarak pushed past his embarrassment and fear and tried to remember.

"There was a sort of a snuffling and scratching sound, like claws on a wall."

CHAPTER 3

"Ah, now we have a wall. Surely there are no walls in 'nothing'. Think, Tarak. Were you inside or outside this wall?"

Tarak thought. "Inside."

"And the scratching?"

"Came from outside."

"Something was trying to get in?"

Tarak nodded. "It was trying to get to me." He broke into a cold sweat. "I was so afraid. I am sorry, Grandmother."

"Sorry? What are you sorry for?" Iri'waw cocked her head.

Tarak fought the tears that welled to his eyes. "For failing on my quest."

The old shaman woman smiled but she did not laugh.

"A Spirit Quest is not a fishing trip, Tarak. You don't either come back with a fish or not. Yours was not a simple vision, but that does not mean it was unimportant. This is a powerful dream but the spirits speak in a language not easily understood. It takes time to discover the layers of meaning. We go on the mountain and cry for a vision, and when we return we must live with what we saw and think about it and then live and think about it some more. It may take a lifetime to understand the vision we have been given and sometimes just when you think you understand it, something else happens and you see everything in a new way. Then you are so amazed, you wonder why you could not see this before? But you were not ready. You did not yet have the understanding. This takes time and years of living." Iri'waw put her wrinkled hand on Tarak's shoulder. "One day light will come into this darkness you saw, Tarak, and you will understand your vision." She sat back. "Next time you dream, come and tell me about it. We will sit outside the cave and talk."

That had been the first time Tarak had gone to Iri'waw's cave. He had been there three more times since then. Now, whenever he dreamed, he made the trek to her cave and told her about it.

The old woman studied his dreams like a hunter studies scat, prodding and poking at them, but whatever she found there, she did not share it with Tarak.

Once when he dreamed during The Moon of the Woka Harvest, Tarak decided not to tell anyone that he had dreamed so that he would not have to go to the cave. When Iri'waw passed by while he was playing with the other boys, she did not even look at him and he was sure he had fooled her. But that evening, after the sun had gone down, she had sent for him.

The only thing worse than going to the dark, smelly cave during the day, was going at night. The trail twisted and turned like a living snake and Tarak was sure axe' ki spirits lurked in the shadows. The trees were full of whispers, and sharp looks from dead eyes jabbed him in the back.

CHAPTER 3

Tarak put a hand on Ghost's back to steady his nerves. Ghost looked up, his bright eyes dancing.

"What are you laughing at?" Tarak pouted. "If you had any sense, you would be scared too." Ghost stepped closer, his side touching Tarak's thigh. Confidence slipped from dog to boy and they went on.

Tarak reached the mouth of the cave and peered inside. Goosebumps chilled his skin. The darkness seemed to push back against the rock walls like a prisoner held against their will. The villagers said Iri'waw talked to the axe' ki. Were the evil spirits here now? Were they looking at him--laughing at him?

Ghost gave a rumbley sort of growl as a spark flared in the gutted eye sockets of a coyote hide draped over a staff in the corner. Tarak stared back at the yellow eyes, his mouth dry, his pulse racing. He took a step back and Iri'waw stepped from the shadows.

"Ah, young Tarak. You have come." Her shell earrings swung as she moved, the tattooed lines on her chin falling into the deep crevices that wrinkled her brown skin. Thin shoulder bones pushed up beneath her leather dress. "You and your old dog."

"Ghost is not old," Tarak bristled. It was true his friend moved more slowly on chilly mornings, but before the sun was far above the ridge, he was again as eager and quick as a pup.

Iri'waw grunted. "Your father brought him to the village before you had seen your third winter and you have now seen what, thirteen? That is not too old for a boy, but not so young for a dog."

Tarak did not like the idea that his friend was getting old. Whenever he imagined his future as a great hunter, Ghost was always there with him. He did not want to think of a life without Ghost and yet the same years that saw Tarak growing taller wore differently on his friend.

"Sometimes people fix their eyes so hard on tomorrow's sunrise that they miss the warmth and beauty of today. Isn't that right, old bear?" Iri'waw sighed as she scratched the base of the dog's pointed ear. "Come, Tarak. We will talk outside tonight."

The old woman's cedar staff thudded against the dirt, stirring the scent of pine needles from the forest duff littering the ground. She shuffled to a rock and sat, quietly waiting, her wrinkled face lifted to the night sky. Her long, white, hair glowed in the starlight. Frog-song drifted up from the river.

"So my young friend, tell me about your dream," she said in her low, throaty voice.

Tarak twisted his fingers, cleared his throat and began.

"The people of our village sat eating in the dark but when the food touched their mouths it disappeared, so everyone was very hungry. I looked up. There was a pathway of stars in the sky

CHAPTER 3

above us, very high and far away, but Ghost led me to a place where the stars touched the earth, all piled up so you could climb them like a ladder. Ghost could not climb and I did not want to leave him, but he smiled at me like he does sometimes, telling me it was okay; he would wait for me. So I climbed up the stars alone until I reached the pathway in the sky.

"After I had walked awhile, I came to a camp where spirits were sitting around a fire, eating and laughing. They looked very fierce but when I looked down, I could see Ghost far below smiling up at me so I was not so afraid. Somehow I knew the fire the spirits sat by was not just a normal fire; it was the fierce one's secret knowledge; a knowledge of many things.

"When the spirits' bellies were full, they fell asleep. I snuck forward and took one of the burning sticks from the fire and ran as fast as I could, climbing back down the stars to where Ghost was waiting. Together we ran back to the village. Mother cooked a feast over the special fire and now the food did not disappear in my people's mouths. They ate and were full and happy again."

Iri'waw studied Ghost as she rubbed her tattooed chin.

"So, the white dog follows you even in your dreams?"

Tarak shrugged. "We go everywhere together."

"Hmm. I have heard this story before. It is told by people far to the North."

"The Takelma?"

"No, farther. Farther even than the Pasqanwas. It is from people that live on the Great River. In their version, human beings have no fire until Coyote steals it from the Spirits of the Sky and gives it to the people. For the people of the Great River, Coyote is a clever trickster, like Mink and his foolish brother, Weasel, in our stories."

"Like the stories of my mother's people?"

"Yes. In these stories Coyote loves to make fun of the other animals, and sometimes people-- especially those who think they are important." Iri'waw turned her keen gaze on Tarak and looked hard at him. "Tarak, do you think you are important?"

Tarak shook his head. "A boy is not important. Only a man." Tarak puffed out his chest, unable to keep the pride from his voice. "A hunter is the most important person in a village."

Iri'waw grunted.

"So when a deer stands so that a hunter's arrow can strike it, you think it is because the hunter is more important than the deer?"

"The hunter must feed his family."

"What about the deer's family? Do they not have needs?"

Tarak did not know how to answer. His grandfather had taught him to respect all living things, but if all life was equally sacred, how could

CHAPTER 3

he say that a human's life was more important than a four-legged's? He looked at Ghost. Ghost was a four-legged and he was more important to Tarak than anything.

"The deer stands because it recognizes its brother's need," Iri'waw explained. "A hunter understands that when a four legged one or a winged one gives their life for his family, it is a gift, not a right. One who does not know this, is not yet a man."

Iri'waw leaned on her stick and rose to her feet.

"When you dream again, come see me--you and your white shadow." She shuffled back to her cave and the darkness swallowed her.

The very next day, Tarak and Ghost had gone hunting and the Snake had taken his deer.

*****

The morning after the Snake had moved on, Tarak woke and washed in the river as usual. Then, he ate and fetched water and wood for his mother.

"These are women's chores," he grumbled, stacking the wood by the fire pit. He was not happy knowing he would be stuck in camp all day. "When I am a man, Little Sister will have to do these things." Ghost flopped down, his eyes following Tarak.

"Your little sister can barely walk," A'ni pounded boiled acorns for the dough she would reboil into mush for their dinner. "I think you can help your mother out a few more years. Stay close to the village today."

"Yes, Mother."

Tarak and Ghost traced the outer limits of the village, his bow and quiver slung over his back in case a deer strayed within bow shot. Ghost's tongue dribbled sloppy, saliva onto the dirt, his snappy black eyes smiling. It didn't matter to the old dog whether he and Tarak went hunting or walked around the village, as long as they were together.

Every path in the village eventually led to the river. It was the center of their lives, providing fish, water for cooking, drinking, washing, and recreation. Tarak and Ghost arrived at the riverbank where his grandfather and cousin were burning and scraping a new dugout canoe. Ghost and Tarak plopped down on the warm sand beside them.

"It is almost finished," Kari-wa, said with pride. "You and I, will soon go fishing in my new canoe, little cousin."

Kari-wa was older than Tarak by four Pik-i-owish re-makings. At dances, all the girls from the other villages made eyes at him, but his parents had not chosen a bride for him yet.

Tarak grunted. "I don't want to go fishing. I want to go hunting."

"Still sulking over your deer?" Kari-wa jabbed Tarak in the ribs.

CHAPTER 3

"Those Snake stole that doe from me." Tarak crossed his arms over his chest, frowning deeply.

"Stole it? Did you have a rope on it then?" Kari-wa teased him. "Were you about to ride it back to the village? I know. You were going to lead it back to camp, put flowers around its neck and name it 'Tarak's Deer'."

"I was not."

"Hmm, who is Tarak's dear? Oh, I know. It is Chiwa'chni. Chiwa'chni is Tarak's dear."

Tarak grabbed Kari-wa's leg and yanked him off balance.

"That's not true. I never said that." Tarak launched himself into his cousin. Wrestling, the boys tumbled over each other in the sun-warmed sand with Ghost barking and bouncing beside them. Puffs of sand flew from the tangle of arms and legs until Kari-wa pinned Tarak.

"I win!" He jumped to his feet.

Tarak sat up shook the sand from his hair and spit it from his mouth.

Kari-wa noticed his grandfather still patiently scraping charcoal from the dugout. Pulling his digging stick from the sand where he had dropped it, he went back to work.

"This old man thinks it is good the Snake only took one deer," A'cmu said, as if nothing had interrupted the conversation. "The Takelma lost many lives when raiders came to their camp this summer."

"Grandfather is right, cousin," Kari-wa agreed, trying to look serious and grown up. "You may not have brought a deer home for the cook-fire but you warned the village." He slapped Tarak on the back. "You are a hero."

"No one treats me like a hero," Tarak complained. "They treat me like a little boy."

"A boy hero." Kari-wa laughed.

Tarak made a face at him.

"Maybe it is not deer my grandson hunts," A'cmu said, quietly.

The boys looked at each other and rolled their eyes. They would dishonor their elder by arguing with him but sometimes old men said the craziest things as if they made perfect sense. Of course, it was deer that Tarak hunted. He needed a deer to become a man.

"Tarak, when you see a man with yellow feathers tied in his hair, what do you think?" his grandfather asked.

"I think he is a brave warrior."

The old man nodded. "The feathers symbolize his courage. But if he were to lose the feathers would he then run and hide?"

Tarak snorted. "Of course not, A'cmu."

"No, of course not." A'cmu smiled. "Because whether he has the feathers or not, he is the same man. Having them did not make him brave and losing them would not make him a coward." The old man stopped scraping and held

CHAPTER 3

his grandson's gaze. "Feathers do not make a warrior any more than a deer makes a man."

A hawk's warning cry shrilled through the canyon. A'cmu looked up, shading his eyes against the sun.

"There are strangers on the ridge."

Kari-wa reached for his bow. "The Snake have come back."

Two figures stood at the edge of the cliff above the village. They wore leather pants, coats and hats with broad brims. "No." A'cmu shook his head. "Not the Snake. They are pas'stin; white men."

CHAPTER FOUR

The afternoon sun grew old, fading into evening then sank behind the ridge, leaving the river valley in a lingering twilight.

Balls of fire hovered above the river, their reflection rippling on the dark water. Village men, working in groups of three, used torchlight to attract fish to the river's surface. One held the torch, balancing the dugout. The second poled the dugout slowly back and forth across the river. The third watched the water, ready with a club and net so when a fish rose to the surface, attracted by the torchlight, he could club it, scoop it up in his net and add it to the catch.

Tarak loved summer feast nights, the nutty smell of camas roots and fresh trout roasting on hot stones in the cook-fires, the chirping song of the grasshoppers, the women talking and laughing as they sliced the trout's pink flesh and lay it over the coal-heated stones.

Tonight was not his man-feast, but it was a celebration. Pas'stin strangers had come to the village bringing news from the outside world. There would be new stories and interesting trades. Children crowded around the fire, staring round-

CHAPTER 4

eyed at the white men seated in the place of honor among the elders.

Tarak did not understand why A'cmu had called the strangers "white". Their faces and hands were not that different from his own people--nut brown and weathered. Only when the man named Loo-ee Barbo stretched his neck out so you could see the hidden skin under his shirt did Tarak understand that where the sun had not touched him, the man's skin was as pale as a plucked bird's. The second man however, looked like everyone else Tarak knew--except for the odd clothes he wore. The white man, Loo-ee Barbo, called this younger man Jimmy Buckeye.

Loo-ee Barbo had thick, brown, curly hair that covered his face from his upper lip to below his chin. His eyes were rain-sky gray and his words came so fast it was like they were chasing each other out of his mouth. The villagers did not understand this fast talk, but they liked to watch his lip-fur move up and down like a fuzzy caterpillar stretched under his nose. The man waved his arms when he talked and the expressions on his face came and went as quick as summer lightening.

"Klatawa teawhit enati illahee. We travel on foot across zee land." Barbo made two fingers on each hand walk across the air, helping the villagers understand what he was saying. "Jimmy and I, mitlite tenas, 'stay just a leettle". We trap swelel, mountain beaver." He pulled in his lower jaw and stuck out his upper teeth, holding his weathered hands up in front of him like paws. The younger children giggled behind their hands. They did not want to be rude but the white man was very funny. He smiled at them, clearly pleased at his effect. "We trade hides, *huy huy* lapel, on *Hyas Chuck,* zee Great River." Barbo pointed at the river then spread his arms as wide as he could. "Big, big water; hyas chuck."

"Ah, Hyas Chuck…" some of the elders nodded. They had heard of the Great River far to the North. Were these the people Iri-waw had told him about? Tarak looked across the fire to where the old woman sat. Hers were the only eyes not looking at the white men's; they were fixed on him.

"I know this story," she had told him. *"It is from people who live on the Great River to the north.* His dream had come from the people of the Hyas Chuck, and now suddenly two travelers from that far away place had stumbled on their small village. What could it mean? Tarak edged closer to Ghost. When he looked up again, Iri'waw had gone.

The younger visitor, Jimmy Buckeye rose, licking berry juice from his fingers and strode away from the fire. Fascinated by the stranger, Tarak followed, Ghost at his side.

Tarak found the visitor sitting on the riverbank near Kari'wa's dugout. He had pulled out a knife and was whittling on a stick of wood.

CHAPTER 4

"Hyas kamooks. That's a big dog." He pointed at Ghost with his chin as he tossed curled shavings.

Tarak smiled, proudly. "That is what everyone says." The stranger's talking words were like the Takelma, whose villages were on a river to the north, and if he paid close attention, Tarak understood his words.

Jimmy reached out a hand to touch Ghost's head but Ghost shrunk back, putting himself out of reach.

Tarak shrugged. "He's friendly once he knows you." Jimmy Buckeye eyed the dugout. "That is my cousin's dugout," Tarak offered.

The fur trader grunted, curling his lip. "It's an overgrown stick. You should see the canoes on the Great River. They fly across the water like giant birds, beautiful and graceful, like softly curled leaves on the water."

"I would like to see such a canoe." Tarak sat cross-legged in the sand opposite Jimmy. The visitor was no more than a handful of winters older than Kari-wa but seemed to know so much more.

"A man from the Takelma visited our village in The Moon After the Floods. His words were like yours. Was he from your village?"

Jimmy shook his head. "I do not live under the White Mountain. I live on the Hyas Chuck; the Great River."

"But you speak like a Takelma—"

"My mother's people." Jimmy shrugged. "She left when she was a girl but she taught me her people's wawa. I am not one of them though. I am a fur trapper for the Hudsons Bay Company and Hyas Tee, the one white men call Doctor McLoughlin. I trap beaver with Loo-ee."

Tarak frowned. "There are not many beaver on our river."

"Then we will not stay long." Jimmy returned to his whittling.

"I am Tarak, and this is Ghost."

The trapper eyed the big dog. "Ghost, eh? On the Great River we say 'skookum'. A dog like that would make a good pack animal. We could use a pack dog to help us move our pelts. You could trade him to me."

Tarak frowned, confused. He wanted the trapper to like him but he could never sell Ghost. He shook his head, putting a protective arm around the dog's shoulders. "I could not. He is a friend."

Disappointment flashed across Jimmy Buckeye's face, he shrugged and turned away as if he did not care but Tarak could see it was not true.

"When we get back to the Great River, Loo-ee and I will get big dolla' from Hyas Tee. We will be big muckamuck men, Loo-ee and I. We will buy lots of nice things and have as many big dogs as we want. When they see the piles and piles of fur pelts we have cached, they will take off their hats to us and show us great respect." The trapper gave the dugout a disgusted look, making sure

CHAPTER 4

Tarak understood that he was the superior man. "Do you know the Fort, Fort Vancouver?" he asked casually.

Tarak shook his head. "My people do not travel so far north."

Jimmy clicked his tongue. "Too bad. Hyas Tee, the great chief of all the white men in the West, lives there. The tillikum call him 'the Great White Headed Eagle'. Loo-ee and I work for him." He stuck his chest out. "He is a giant, taller than any living man, but his children are sitkum siwash: half-Indian, like me."

Tarak swallowed. "Is this Hyas Tee an axe' ki?" He whispered the name of the powerful spirits his people believed made them sick.

Jimmy Buckeye snorted, shaking his head at Tarak's ignorance. "No. Axe' ki are like tenas tillikum, little children, to Hyas Tee. The Great White Headed Eagle has hyas tamanawas; big power. When he speaks, things get done. All the tillikum listen to him; Boston men, King Georgemen, Siwash, and the Klale men with the black skin."

"There are so many kinds of people?" Tarak asked in awe.

"Nawitka." Buckeye nodded. "And Hyas Tee is muckamuck above them all." He poked his thumb into his chest. "He gives Loo-ee and me many fine blankets, sugar, beef meat--whatever we want, because our pelts are kloshe, good.

Kumptus? Loo—ee and me go klatawa, everywhere, see everything. We are free men."

"I would like to... klatawa." Tarak rolled the new word over his tongue. It tasted exciting, like faraway places and adventures where men were brave and their lives could turn in an instant to danger. He was sure these men never had to haul water or wood like girls.

A slow smile widened Jimmy Buckeye's mouth and he glanced at Ghost. "Kloshe. You pick up the jargon pretty good. Maybe you and the big, white kamooks should come trapping with us, eh? I could wawa to Loo-ee for you. But you would have to mamook very hard with the traps, kumptus? You understand? We no ticky lazy siwashs and the big kamooks would have to work too. Everybody has to pull their weight when you're trapping. It is hard work."

Tarak's heart leapt. "I can mamook hard. I will ask my mother tonight if I can go with you."

Jimmy's mouth twisted and he tossed the stick he had been carving on into the water. "Only a boy has to ask his mother to go klatawa. We cannot take a boy with us. Trapping is a man's job."

Tarak's chin jutted up. "I will have my first hunt soon--tomorrow maybe. Then I will be a man and I will not have to ask anyone to do anything."

"If you have your first hunt tomorrow your back side will be sore for a week from the

CHAPTER 4

bowstring lashes the men will give you to welcome you among them." Jimmy laughed as he stood.

"It won't hurt me," Tarak boasted. The lashing was another part of the man-making ritual. Everyone tried to make it sound worse than it was but the lashing was only symbolic and not meant to hurt.

"Well, whatever you do, it will have to be soon." Jimmy sniffed, beginning to head back toward the feast. "Because if there are no beaver, we will not stay."

That night Tarak begged and pleaded with his father and mother but Ata' would not give in. He would not let his son go hunting, or travel North with the fur trappers. The Snake might still be near and a party of three men and a dog would be easy prey.

Three days after the Hudson's Bay men came to the village, Loo-ee Barbo and Jimmy Buckeye walked up the trail headed north. Tarak and Ghost watched them until there was nothing left to see.

CHAPTER FIVE

Tarak climbed up the short ladder that connected his family's lodge with the ground level and stepped out into the morning. Ghost ran to greet him, his pink tongue hanging over his black lips, his mouth curled up at the edges in a broad, doggy smile. His fur hung in heavy, wet, spikes and his legs were caked with mud. He had already been to the river. Circling Tarak, the dog nipped playfully at the boy's loincloth.

"I'm coming. I'm coming," Tarak laughed.

Summer, fall, winter or spring, the Kama'twa bathed in the Klamath. A'cmu said it made their body's strong and kept sickness away. Men of the village also purified themselves in the sweat house, singing songs and drumming. Only the axe' ki spirits, who shot pains into humans, could make the strong people of the river sick.

"Mother, it's been five days since the Snake came," Tarak began the speech he had been rehearsing. "They will be far away by now."

"Perhaps." A'ni rubbed fine, red, dust off her paint stone, mixing it with water and duck's blood. It made a deep, rich red paint. Tarak's little sister copied her mother, mixing dirt and water and painting great stripes of mud on her legs. A'ni took

CHAPTER 5

a stiff reed brush and began tracing a pattern of stars along the edge of a white leather hide cut out in the shape of a shirt. The neat row of stars stood out handsomely against the creamy buckskin.

"It is a good shirt," Tarak complimented his mother's skill.

"I hope its wearer will find it so." His mother painted the red stars in groups of five, a sacred number to their people. Sitting back on her heels, she examined her work. "But I think I have cut it too small for your father's shoulders." She sighed. "Even so, I might as well finish it. Who knows? Someone else may need a new shirt for a special occasion soon." She smiled up at Tarak.

She had made the shirt for him. Tarak knew it. He felt like the sun had just broken through the clouds to shine in one spot and that was on him. "It really is a very, very nice shirt, Mother," he said again, kissing her cheek. "Whoever you give it to will be very proud to wear it."

"Hmmm. The hunters saw a patch of ripe berries downriver. Some of the mothers wanted to send their girls gathering but they were still worried about raiders. I told them I would ask if you wanted to go along to look after them."

"I would. Thank you, Mother!" It was not a man's job, but it was not a child's chore either and the best part was it was away from the village. He might see a deer. He might bring one home today.

"Ghost! We're going hunting today!" Tarak called out as he raced to the riverbank. "Woo-hoo!"

E.F. WINTERS

Shouting and barking, the two friends splashed into the sparkling water.

Before the sun had reached the peak of Wai-i-ka, Tarak and Ghost were leading the berrying party down river. Ghost walked happily alongside the children, stopping and waiting when Chiwa'chni, the smaller of the two girls, fell behind. Ti'caw hurried to catch up with Tarak.

"We heard you almost shot a deer, Tarak. It is too bad you missed."

Tarak frowned. He had not missed. He had not even shot his bow. He was sure Ti'caw knew that and also knew why, but she was just an annoying girl and never pleasant; like her namesake, the hornet.

Ti'caw was really the worst sort of girl. She had a wide flat nose, small, squinty eyes, and she never stopped talking. It didn't even matter to her whether what she said was true or not. The words just spilled out like accidents and when they were wrong, or poorly chosen, she ignored it, pretending she was not responsible. Tarak glanced back at Chiwa'chni. Her name meant flower. Her small, graceful hand rested gently on Ghost's back as they walked silently along the river. Chiwa'chni hardly ever said anything. If there had to be girls; that was the best kind.

"Why did you bring a bow with you, Tarak?" Ti'caw giggled behind her hand. "Are you going to shoot the berries off the bush? Chiwa'chni," she called back over her shoulder.

CHAPTER 5

"Tarak is going to shoot the berries off the bush! What a clever idea." She peeked into Tarak's quiver. "But Tarak, with such big arrowheads there won't be anything left to eat."

"A bow and arrow are not for berries, Ti'caw," Tarak grumped. "They are for hunting."

"Well, there won't be any hunting today. It's not allowed." Ti'caw skipped ahead. "My mother said you were not supposed to go off on your own. She said that you have to stay with us. Anyway, I don't see any hunters around here. Do you, Chiwa'chni? I only see a foolish boy with a swelled head."

Tarak swallowed. Ti'caw was good at word games. He never saw her traps until it was too late and he always said the wrong thing. She seemed to take personal pleasure in shaming him.

"I brought my bow and arrows because I was asked to protect you," Tarak said sullenly.

Ti'caw's laugh was like bitter poison. "Protect us? From what, thorns? You must not tell stories except during the snow moons, Tarak. You will make the rattlesnakes angry." She made a hissing-rattling sound.

"You sound more like a Grandma with missing teeth than a rattlesnake," Tarak spat back.

"Stupid boy, don't you understand? Our mothers were just being polite. Your mother asked if you could come with us so the men could go hunting without you scaring all the deer away."

Ti'caw flipped a black braid over her shoulder and stuck her nose in the air.

Tarak blushed. It wasn't true. He was sure it wasn't, but he hated that she'd said it.

"With a tongue like yours, Ti'caw, you don't need protection." Tarak gripped his bow tight in his fist. "You could just talk the raiders to death. Come on, Ghost." He stalked off up the bank. Ghost hesitated, looking at Chiwa'chni, but turned and followed his friend.

Tarak climbed through the grove of trees that lined the river's edge, crossed a meadow and was headed into the oak woods on the other side before he looked back. The girls had been swallowed up by the brush but they had found the berries. He could see the tops of one of their heads as they reached out to pick the ripe fruit. Ti'caw's chatter echoed off the hills like a scolding squirrel.

"Stupid, noisy girl," he grumped. "They can probably hear her all the way back in the village." Ghost whimpered. "They're fine. We can watch over them from here," Tarak reassured Ghost and himself, beginning to feel a little guilty now that he was not in the heat of his argument with Ti'caw. No matter how unpleasant her sharp tongue was, he had said he would protect her and stomping off into the woods was not a very grown-up way to do that. "We will stay away just long enough to scare that nasty hornet," he told Ghost. "Once she realizes they are alone and helpless without us maybe she will hold her tongue and be a little nicer."

CHAPTER 5

Something startled a crow from the oak trees to their right. Ghost's ears pricked up like teepees. Boy and dog scanned the grove. Something larger than a man--larger even than a bear, stood on four legs beneath the trees. Tarak held his breath. An icy shiver climbed his spine.

Axe' ki.

Six demons were lined up at the edge of the grove, their knobby legs the size of saplings, their necks as thick as a man's body. Their heads looked as if they had been stretched from front to back then squashed flat and along their necks was a stiff ridge of coarse hair. Matching tails whipped the air behind them. Rock-like feet danced in place as if the demons wanted to run but were being held back by some invisible hand.

With a whoop, one burst free, running so fast it was as if it flew across the meadow. Tarak gasped. From the middle of the creature's back a second, smaller body appeared: a body with the head and arms of a man. The demon turned and headed for the berry patch.

Ghost yelped as he sprang into motion.

"No, Ghost!" Tarak reached out. But he was too late. Ghost raced the demon, running toward Chiwa'chni.

Cries from upriver shredded the afternoon stillness.

"Mother...father." Tarak froze in fear. *The village.* Axe'ki were not only here in the meadow; they were attacking the village.

One of the demons threw back its man head and gave a full-throated battle cry. "Ay-yiy!"

The girls' heads popped up out of the bushes like ground squirrels. Their baskets dropped, and they blundered out of the berry patch, running upriver towards the village, their frightened screams emptying their lungs.

"No! Stop! Don't go back!" Tarak tried to warn them but the terrified girls heard only their own panic. As Tarak sprinted downhill, two more demons leapt from the trees. One swerved toward him.

Ahead, a white blur leapt at the demon closing in on the girls. An arrow whirred through the air and Ghost fell like a stone.

"No!" Fear ripped Tarak's throat as he began to run toward his fallen friend.

A demon's ear-splitting shriek clawed at his back. The ground under his feet rumbled like thunder beneath the weight of the demon's feet, its hot breath exploding against the back of his neck in sharp puffs. The shadow the axe'ki cast on the ground reached out for Tarak and he twisted sideways, dodging left then right. Stopping, and then changing direction again and again, Tarak zigzagged through the field like a rabbit. The demon was not as agile but it was faster. It could not stay with him every step but if it anticipated a move, it could block him. Closer and closer it came until once again the man arms reached out. Tarak threw himself to the ground, curled into a ball and

CHAPTER 5

rolled through the tall grass. Scrambling on hands and knees, he crawled toward the cover of a clump of sage bushes and pulled himself into a tight ball.

He could not catch his breath. Where should he go? He tried to focus his mind. Where? Not the village, it was not safe there. He pushed a greater understanding of what that meant for his family to the back of his mind. He could not think about that right now-not now.

And what about the girls? Where were they? Could he find them? Could he get to them? Everything was moving too fast. The world they had started out in this morning had become a far more dangerous place than the children could ever have understood.

A girl's voice screamed and Tarak peeked out from his hiding place to see Chiwa'chni running across the lower end of the meadow, a demon on her heels. Shrieking, the frail girl looked back over her shoulder, stumbled, and fell. The demon's stone feet trampled her, kicking her small body out behind it as if it were no more than a straw doll.

Tarak stared at the place she had fallen, unable to make sense of it. They had just gone berry picking that was all. It had been a lazy summer day like any other summer day and now the world had turned upside down.

The ground shook like Grandmother Earth had swallowed a storm and was trying to belch it back out.

In the lower meadow, the axe' ki had found a new target.

"Ti'caw! Behind you!" Tarak shouted.

When the man-arms reached out to grab the pudgy girl, she slapped at them, hard.

"Leave me alone!" she shouted, barely breaking her stride. The demon hesitated, threw back its man head and laughed, but before the laugh's echo had faded, the creature was back in the chase.

Ti'caw swerved and dodged and struck anything that came near her, but all her courage only gained her a few more moments of freedom. The axe-ki circled wide, came back around and lifted her off the ground, ignoring her angry fists. Slinging the girl across its broad back, the demon disappeared into the trees. One of its companions scooped up the limp form of Chiwa'chni and followed.

Suddenly the meadow was still.

Tracks of sweat striped the dust that coated Tarak's skin. Distant cries from the village rose with the black smoke, making a dark smudge across the blue sky. Tarak's heart felt like a stone in his chest--too heavy and cold to breathe around.

"Ghost," he sobbed. He needed to get to Ghost. Forcing himself to his feet, Tarak stumbled through the grass and scrub brush, searching for the other half of himself.

Laying flat on the trampled grass, Ghost panted hard and fast, the effort of each breath

CHAPTER 5

moving his whole body. Sticky lines of blood oozed across his white fur, coming from a hole where an arrow still stuck out of his side. The dog's eyes were clouded with pain but he tried to lift his huge head to greet Tarak.

"Don't move, boy," Tarak warned him. Ghost dropped his head back down, unable to do anything more. "You're going to be all right, old bear. You're going to be all right." Tarak scrabbled through the grass to find something to bind the wound. "I'll get you home. Iri'waw and Mother will know what to do. They'll heal you up as good as new." He sniffled, wiping his eyes. What would he find back at the village? Was his mother even alive? Was Iri'waw? Were any of those he knew and loved?

"Everything will be fine," he said, as if just saying it could make it true. Ata' and the other men were strong warriors. If they had returned, they would have protected the village and any minute now one of them would come into the meadow.

Tarak plucked sage leaves from one of the bushes. "Forgive me, little sister. I have no offering to give you, but I need your help." He turned back to Ghost. Gently sweeping the fur away from the arrow shaft, he examined the wound. The stone head was not buried deep. Its flared edges had struck a rib, stopping it from entering the softer flesh. "This is going to hurt," Tarak warned. Gritting his teeth, he pulled the arrow out. He crushed the sage leaves, and covered the wound pressing down gently to stop the bleeding.

"Good boy. See, that was not so bad, eh? You're a strong old bear. Nothing can stop you." He rested his head against his friend's furry neck. "Please, be okay. Please, don't leave me."

Focused on his friend, Tarak had not felt the ground begin to rumble again or heard the hard fall of the demon's stone feet.

A hand gripped his arm and yanked him into the air.

"Ghost!"

Ghost and the ground fell away. Tarak felt a sharp pain on the back of his head and the world went black.

CHAPTER SIX

Tarak kept his head low, studying his captors from behind the curtain of his hair. They were not axe'ki demons with two heads and men's bodies. They were Snake raiders, riding on the backs of four-leggeds called horses. He had heard about such animals, just as he had heard about white men, but he had never seen one, until now. But axe'ki or not, they had taken him and they were not letting him go; he nor the others.

Tarak looked down the short line of boys and the much longer line of women the Snake had taken prisoner. There were more than he could count on the fingers of both hands but he knew less than half of them. Other villages had been raided and now they had all been gathered together to travel north.

Chiwa'chni and Ti'caw had been tied into the women's line so he could not always see them, but when he did catch a glimpse, it worried him. Chiwa'chni wove unsteadily as she walked, the left side of her face swollen and bruised. A large woman, not from their village, was tied between her and Ti'caw, and she helped Ti'caw pull the smaller girl along.

A few of the women carried babies in cradleboards on their backs. Others struggled along with toddlers too old for cradleboards but not sure or steady enough on their feet to keep up the pace the Snake set. Their mothers carried them as long as they could then other's stepped in and took a turn.

The captives were connected like human beads strung together on a rope, making them easy to guard but making it hard to travel. Branches whipped their faces, roots grabbed at their feet and stones rose from the ground to trip them. When one prisoner fell, everyone in the line was pulled off balance, but whatever injuries they suffered, the Snake pressed on. These were not their lands. They needed to put distance between their captives and any chance they could be rescued.

"Yumis, the next time one of the Snake comes close, we should attack him," Tarak whispered to the boy on his right. Yumis was not the bravest or boldest boy in their village but he was no coward.

"Do you have a bow and arrow, Tarak?" he stared at Tarak in disbelief." Do you have a knife? No, because the Snake took them. How are we supposed to fight?"

"You saw what they did to that old auntie when she refused to walk," a boy from another village whispered. "If we make trouble they, will beat us."

CHAPTER 6

Tarak lifted his chin. "Are we not men? A man must fight."

Yumis grunted. "If we were men, we would be dead. We are only alive because when the Snake look at us they see boys. Raiders don't take men captive, Tarak. They kill them. Men are too much trouble to keep alive."

"No wawa. Mahish klatawa." A guard on a tall horse motioned them to keep walking. They obeyed, wondering what he had heard, their hearts pounding.

It is a dream, Tarak told himself, wishing he could wake up. He would not even mind going to Iri'waw's cave to tell her about it if only it would be a dream and he could wake up in his own bed with Ghost beside him. Was his friend all right? Had someone from the village gone looking for the children and found the big white dog? Was there anyone left who would care? Tarak thought about his father, mother and sisters.

"Please, let them be safe," he prayed as he trudged on.

The sun dipped behind the western mountains and the Snake turned their prisoners north, away from Wai-i-ka.

The day had been warm when they left the village to go berrying but now the night wind blowing off the snow capped mountain chilled Tarak's half-bare body. Looking back over his shoulder, he checked on Ti'caw and Chiwa'chni in the women's line. If he had been with them in the berry patch would the raiders have found them? If he had been where he was supposed to be, could he have kept Ti'caw quiet and led them to a hiding place? Shame burned his cheeks. If he had done what he had been sent to do, they might not be here now.

The Snake stopped them at the edge of a stone field so they could wrap the horse's feet with leather to protect them form the rough volcanic stones. Yumis looked up at the darkening sky.

"No one is coming for us."

"You're wrong. They will need to put things together first. It will take time, but they will come," Tarak insisted.

"Did you see the village?" Yumis asked, scornfully.

"No," Tarak answered, quietly.

"Then do not speak to me of putting things together, like this was a windstorm."

"They will not leave us," Tarak said firmly.

"It's too late, Tarak. Even if they had enough men who were not wounded to try, they could not track us across the stone field." A glazed look came over his eyes. "We will never see our parents again. We are dead to them, now."

Tarak turned his head and looked back. Dark ridges of trees lined up one behind the other. Somewhere among them was his village, burned and broken. Somewhere on a hillside above it, Ghost lay bleeding. Tarak's throat closed and he

CHAPTER 6

forced back tears. His enemies would not see him cry.

"I am not dead. I will come home. I will find a way," he vowed under his breath.

A coyote yipped in the distance. It sounded like the mischievous spirit was laughing.

CHAPTER SEVEN

Ghost wiped his eyes with his paw and looked around. It was night. Darkness covered the world. He was lying on the grass beside a sage bush on a hillside down river from the village. Where was Tarak? The big, white dog raised his nose and sniffed the breeze. The smoke on the air smelled of sadness. The familiar sounds and smells of village life were gone, replaced by the cries of women mourning their dead, and the strong scent of burnt wood.

Danger. Ghost tried to stand but a sharp pain buckled his legs and he fell back onto the flattened grass. When the world stopped spinning, he raised his head again, this time more cautiously. A patch of stars glimmered above him and he could see spirits gathering there; A'cmu, the neighbor woman and her baby, a few elders and some of Ata's friends. The wind moved through their transparent bodies, rippling them like water.

"Boof! Boof!" Ghost barked at them, pain stabbing his side like a knife.

A'cmu looked down from the sky. "We travel to the Spirit Land tonight. Will you be coming with us, Old Bear?" He stretched his hand out toward the dog.

CHAPTER 7

Confusion washed over Ghost and he whimpered, searching for Tarak. Where was his boy?

"Tarak will not be coming with us," A'cmu answered. "His path lies another way." He looked north.

Ignoring the pain, Ghost willed himself to his feet. The crushed sage leaves Tarak had placed over his wound fell onto the trampled grass.

"If you come with us, the pain will stop," A'cmu told the white dog. "But you will have to leave Tarak behind."

Ghost sniffed the spot on the ground where Tarak had knelt beside him and puled softly. Tarak had been there, but something had taken him away. He marked the unfamiliar scent of the horse and began to limp across the meadow, tracking it.

A'cmu's spirit turned back to the others and they began their journey along the star path to the West.

Ghost followed the horse's trail through the grass into the oak grove to the ridgeline. From the edge of the cliff above the village he could see the dark orange skeletons of burning lodges glowing in the dark. The hunched shapes of the raid's survivors sorted through rubble or tended to the wounded and grieving. Ghost could not see the tears that striped the soot on their faces, but he felt them. His mournful howl echoed across the canyon.

Iri'waw looked up, searching the ridge until she found the white dog's body glowing against the night sky.

"Where is your boy, old bear?" She sent the question to him on a breeze.

Ghost puled, looking north. Iri'waw followed his gaze.

"So, they have taken him." She had tried to understand the mystery of the darkness that Tarak had been shown. She had even added her voice to his pleas that he be allowed to go North with the trappers, sensing there was some reason the boy was meant to go. But Ata' and A'ni had clung to their son, insisting he was too young. Now, powers greater than any of them had stepped in; the boy had gone North.

"And what will you do?" Iri'wa asked the old dog.

Ghost turned and began to make his way down the hill, heading north. He would do what he had always done: he would follow Tarak.

CHAPTER EIGHT

Tarak's feet bled into the earth as the Snake pushed them on through the night. By dawn even the horses' heads hung low.

When the first rays of the morning sun touched his face, he felt the numb despair that had held him in its grip. It was as if all the color had been sucked from the world, leaving it in shades of grey. He thought about his family and Ghost, and it was like a piece of him had been torn away. How did a person heal from such a wound? Was it even possible? He wished he and Ghost could walk to Iri'wa's cave and ask the old woman, or that he could sit by his mother's cookfire and speak to her about it. It would be good to sit by the river with A'cmu and Karai'wa while they worked on the dugout. Even if he did not talk, grandfather's silence held many answers. But there was no one now for him to ask.

A strangled cry from the women's line drew Tarak's attention.

"Chiwa'chni!" Ti'caw shouted as the injured girl fell forward. The big woman pulled the line along with her as she jumped forward trying to catch Chiwa'chni and cushion her fall but the rope slowed her and she was too late. With a sickening crack, Chiwa'chni's head struck the ground. The confused line of women fell in a tangle of arms and legs.

A puddle of blood made a dark soup in the dirt around Chiwa'chni's head.

"Chiwa'chni, get up." Ti'caw glanced fearfully ahead. "Chiwa'chni!"

Big Woman leaned down and touched the injured girl's misshapen face.

The Snake leader turned to see why the line had stopped.

"She's not moving," Ti'caw choked out the words. "She's not moving. What should we do?"

Big Woman bumped Ti'caw out of the way with her hip and lifted Chiwa'chni into her fleshy arms.

The Snake leader trotted back toward them.

"Mahish Klatawa!" He shouted. The women shrank from him as he rode by -- all but those near Big Woman. She held her place like an anchor. The Snake eyed her, Chiwa'chni, draped over her arms, blood dripping from the gash in her already swollen head.

"Kimta opoots: leave her." He pointed to the ground in disgust.

Big Woman did not move.

"Kimta opoots!" he repeated, more loudly. Big Woman turned and began to walk, carrying Chiwa'chni, pulling the other women with her.

The Snake leapt from his horse, sliding his knife from its sheath. Blocking the defiant

CHAPTER 8

woman's way, he cut Chiwa'chni from the line. Jerking her from Big Woman's arms, he dragged Chiwa'chni to the side of the trail.

"Kimta opoots." He dropped her in the dirt. Turning back to the others, he made a cutting motion across his throat. "Nawitka laly. Cultus." His words were unfamiliar but the message was clear; Chiwa'chni no longer had any value to the Snake.

Ti'caw paled. "No. Please, don't leave my friend. Please. I'll take care of her, I promise. She won't be any trouble. I promise. Please!" she wailed.

Big Woman set her jaw, took a deep breath, stomped back and picked the little girl up out of the dirt, pulling the women tied to her along behind.

"I will carry her."

The Snake's face went red and he charged, shoving his shoulder into the captive woman's stomach. As she doubled over, he pulled Chiwa'chni from her again, tossing her back onto the ground.

"Alta!" He glared at Big Woman, pulling her back to the other half of the line and tying her firmly. She glared back, defiantly. He took his knife and drew it across her neck, barely touching the skin.

"Alta!" The Snake pushed the women's line into motion.

Thrusting her chin into the air, Big Woman walked on, cursing under her breath.

"No. Please. No!" Ti'caw's feet made drag marks in the dirt as the women pulled her forward. "Chiwa'chni!" The Snake hit her.

"I am a stone," Tarak thought to himself. *"I am a stone and stones do not cry."*

******

It was twilight on the second day before the captives were given time to rest. The youngest guard walked the lines, giving out small strips of dried jerky while his companions looked to their horses and their own needs. It was the first food they had been given since they were captured and it could have tasted like bark and been welcome. Some of the prisoners gobbled the strips of meat quickly, while others seemed past noticing it was even there, staring as if they no longer saw this world.

Ti'caw's face was streaked with dirt and tears.

"Ti'caw," Tarak said quietly. "I am sorry about Chiwa'chni."

Ti'caw turned to Big Woman. "Auntie, did you hear something?"

Big Woman thrust her tattooed chin in Tarak's direction.

"The little man said he was sorry for your friend."

Ti'caw's lips puckered and she spit on the ground. "There are no men here. If there were,

CHAPTER 8

Chiwa'chni would not have been left behind." She turned to Tarak, fresh tears wetting her face. "You should have brought a basket to go berrying, Tarak. Then maybe you would have been of some use. Where were you and your bow when the Snake ran us down? You were supposed to protect us," she shouted. "You wanted to prove you were a man? You are not a man. You are just a selfish little boy, and because of you, Chiwa'chni is dead." She spat again.

The other prisoners looked away. This was not their growl.

Tarak hugged his knees and closed his eyes, but it did not shut out Ti'caw's words. They had been in his own mind for many miles now.

"Eat." A foot nudged him as slices of dried meat dropped into his lap.

Tarak did not move.

"If you do not eat, you will get weak. Then it will be you who is left beside the trail." The young guard stood looking down at Tarak. "We may not have power over everything that happens to us, but we can choose how we face it." Like Jimmy Buckeye, the guard spoke in words that Tarak could understand if he listened carefully.

Yumis wolfed down his jerky. "You speak words like the Kama'twa. Who are your people?"

The guard squatted beside the boys. He was not much older than they were, but tall and lanky.

"My mother and I were taken from our village on the east side of the Great White

Mountain when I was a baby. I was raised by the Numa, but my mother sometimes speaks to me in the words of her birth people."

Bitterness soured Tarak's empty belly. "You are a slave to the Snake and now you help them steal the lives of others?"

The young guard lifted his head. "I am not a slave. I have earned a place among The People. My mother is the wife of an elder. We are Numa now. When I became a man, I was given a Numa name. Everyone who is captured does not stay a slave. Some have the courage to earn a place of honor no matter how they come to their people."

Anger smoldered in Tarak's heart. "The Snake are not your people. They stole your life just like they stole ours. You are not one of them, no matter how you try to fool yourself. This life you are so proud of is only a shadow life."

The young guard picked up one of the pieces of jerky he had dropped for Tarak and bit into it. "Eat and live, or throw it away and see how pride fills your belly. It doesn't matter to me, either way."

"He is right," Big Woman said quietly. "Our old lives are gone. We do not know what is ahead but we must eat to survive, or starve and be left behind to die."

"'Better to die on the trail than live as a slave," Ti'caw retorted.

Big Woman shook her head. "You are young and prideful, little hornet, but you will see;

CHAPTER 8

life is precious. However hard things get, as long as we live, there is hope for us." She took the jerky from one of the dazed women, bit off a piece and pushed it into the woman's mouth. "Chew," she commanded. She turned to Tarak. "Did you hear the Numa boy? Wherever we are taken, if you show courage and a good heart, you may become free again. So eat." She tossed her chin at one of the other women. "You, feed that one beside you." She pointed to another woman who looked as if her mind were fogged by shock. "And do not try to take her food for yourself. I will know."

Reluctantly, Tarak picked up the jerky and took a bite. It had been hastily dried over a fire the way hunters cured meat when they were too far from home and could not carry it back to their village to be cured. Chewing it released the strong gamey flavor of venison. The meat was still soft, cured only a few days ago over a fire.

It was his deer, Tarak realized; the deer the Snake had stolen from him; the deer that would have made him a man. No meat had ever tasted better.

CHAPTER NINE

Ghost woke shivering. Even in the lowlands he now felt the sharp edge of the first frost. Hunger was hollowing his belly and dulling his mind. The pain in his side had become an ache that stabbed him with sharp shocks whenever he moved too fast but in the weeks since he had become separated from Tarak, he had struggled on, following the scent of the horses and the children.

When he found Chiwa'chni beside the trail buzzards had already pecked at her swollen face, releasing the swelling. Ghost's approach scattered them, black wings flapping into the sky.

He prodded her hand with his nose, but she did not pet him. He smelled her mouth and knew she did not breathe. Lying down beside the little girl's body he waited for someone to come and take her home. He waited all day.

When no one came, he rose stiffly and slowly walked on.

He all but lost the scent at the stone field but a thin trail of urine left by a toddler from the village had led him on. A tangle of hair pulled out by a tree branch, a bit of skin scraped off by a rock; the trail had continued; a trail only a dog could

CHAPTER 9

follow. Even so, each day Ghost had fallen farther and farther behind.

He could no longer move quick enough to catch up, or hunt to feed himself, and he would not rest long enough to heal. The flesh began to shrink from his spine, his backbone poking up through his white coat like a snow covered ridge. No longer a well fed member of a loving family, a slow mouse or squirrel had become a treat. Finding a clot of grubs was a lifeline, and with winter on its way, even these small meals would soon be hard to find.

Ghost twisted his head around to clean the pus from his wound. It was hot and tender to the touch, and it smelled bad. He looked around at the forest, his bushy white eyebrows drawing together and whimpered softly. Where were the people? He had always lived with people and they had always cared for him, but there was no one to do that now.

He struggled to get to his feet and failed. He had no strength left. He could go no further.

Blinking into the sun, Ghost felt it warm his fur. It felt good to just lie still. He rested his head on his paws and closed his eyes, drifting back into memories where he and Tarak ran side by side, splashing into the clear water of the Klamath River.

The smell of wood smoke, venison jerky and chicory tea tickled Ghost's nose. Men's voices spoke nearby. Cautiously, he opened one eye then the other, peering out from under bushy eyebrows. The fur trappers who had visited the village sat eating by a fire. Ghost raised his head.

"Zee big one eez awake, mon ami." Loo-ee Barbo said, keeping his voice steady so as not to frighten the dog.

"Hey, old kamooks, feeling better? I bet you're hungry." Jimmy Buckeye broke off a piece of biscuit and leaned toward the big dog.

Ghost tried to stand and back away but something stronger than his weakness stopped him. Ropes cross tied between a tree and a travois held him back. He gave a low, warning growl.

"Be careful," Loo-ee warned. "He might bite your fingers off."

Jimmy held still, the biscuit outstretched toward the dog. "Food will tame him. You'll see. He just needs a chance to get used to us is all. Isn't that right, old kamooks? Once you get to know where your food comes from, you'll be as friendly as a trader looking for a good deal."

Ghost's mouth watered and his stomach gurgled. Fear wrestled with his instinct to survive. He needed to eat. He needed to rest and have his wound cared for. He did not want the man to touch him but he wanted to live.

Jimmy waited, patiently. He had recognized the big dog the moment he saw him on the trail, starving, wounded and almost dead. It had been a bizzare stroke of luck, as if the dog was meant to be his.

Ghost's dry lips pulled back as he reached out to take the salty biscuit. Jimmy let him have it, staying close as the dog bolted the food down.

CHAPTER 9

"See, I'm not going to hurt you," he said softly as he brought out another biscuit, holding it out like the first. "I am going to take care of you, and you are going to take care of our furs." Piece by piece, Jimmy hand fed Ghost, adding bits of dried jerky once he was sure the dog could keep it down. Then he brought out a wooden bowl and put water in it. Ghost lapped it up thirstily.

"Just look at the size of him, Loo-ee. When he's all healed up, he'll pull that travois like a horse."

"Just as long as he doesn't eat like one. Meantime, we haf to pull hees highness around until he heals."

Jimmy reached out to pet the big dog's head. Ghost flinched but he did not pull away.

"Good boy. Good boy," Jimmy said, letting his hands move to the dog's back. "He's strong, Loo-ee. He'll bounce back fast. You'll see," Jimmy reassured his partner. "You are a trapping dog now, eh, kamooks? I think I will call you Skookum. What do you think, Loo-ee?"

Ghost looked north, sadness clouding his dark eyes.

"Yes, that's it, you're Skookum now."

CHAPTER TEN

The captives heard the Great River for a mile before they saw it. The water roared like a living beast.

It was the last salmon run of the year at the Silaylo Falls fishery. Dotted with stands of oak, the dry, summer grasslands sloped gently to the river's shores. All across the wide river, salmon leapt into the air, trying to jump the falls, driven to return to their birthplace and spawn a new generation. Native fishermen on wooden platforms stood with their legs braced against the weight of their huge nets, the mist from the falls rising so thick around them that they looked like they were standing in the clouds.

Up and down the riverbank, native women gutted and filleted strips of pink-fleshed fish, placing the meat on willow-rod racks to dry, while children raced between the rows, shooing away the birds that swooped in to steal a bite.

On the banks above the fishery, a tent city of teepees and canvas army style tents, used by the Europeans who worked for the Hudson's Bay Company had grown up.

CHAPTER 10

Yumis edged closer to Tarak, his eyes wide with both excitement and uncertainty. "There are so many people."

"This is nothing." The young Numa guard dismissed the camp's size. "This is the end of the fishing season. Most people are already packing to go to their winter villages. But the gathering at the spring salmon runs down river; now that is something to see."

"Mitlite," one of the guards ordered the captives, making the sign to sit.

There were fewer of them now. After Chiwa'chni, four more had been abandoned beside the trail. The smallest children had been sold off quickly in villages along the way. They slowed the pace, causing problems among the women, and the Numa were eager to be rid of them. Tarak had been surprised by the pile of goods each had brought.

"A slave bought for one horse at the big water of the Klamath is worth two on the Great River," the young Numa had told Tarak and Yumis.

"But they are only babies," Tarak marveled.

"They will grow up among their new people and understand their ways. They will not be strangers."

Like the Numa guard, these children's hearts and loyalties would belong to those they remembered, not the forgotten faces of faded memories.

Tarak had gone downriver with Ti'caw and Chiwa'chni in the last days before the new Moon of Drying Berries. By his count, it was late in The Moon of Dances now. While they traveled, Pik-i-owish had come and gone. How had the ceremony to re-make the world gone this year? Would it make any difference to him so far away? It was hard to believe that this was the same world as the one he knew beneath the shadow of Wai-i-ka.

In spite of what the Numa guard said, Tarak and the other captives were in awe of the late season gathering at the fishery. People from up and down the Great River and beyond had come to trade whatever they had enough of, for whatever they still needed to get them through the winter. All around them people displayed their trade goods on blankets spread out on the ground; store-bought clothes, tools made of white man's metal, trade blankets and iron pots from the Hudson's Bay Company, red pipestone and buffalo hides from the Plains Tribes, slaves from the Great Basin and the South Coast, and stacks of dried and pounded "sugar salmon".

"These are wealthy people," Yumis marveled. "They wear dentalia shells everywhere." The precious shells decorated arms, noses, ears, necklaces and leather hair wraps.

"There are many villages here." Tarak stared at the designs in feathers, beads, porcupine quills, and elk's teeth that decorated the different styles of clothing. Copper colored chins, cheeks,

CHAPTER 10

arms and chests bore different tribal tattoos. The hair of men and women was either worn in two long braids or hung loose in long, gleaming waves. Hats were popular; raccoon, coyote, floppy wide-brimmed ones, like Loo-ee Barbo and Jimmy Buckeye had worn, and others that fit tight to the head with no brim at all. Some older girls wore brimless, woven hats with strings of small shells falling in a fringe in front of their faces. The shells clicked together softly, swaying in rhythm with the girl's steps.

Tarak's heart stopped as he caught sight of a woman wearing a cone shaped basket hat like the women wore in his village.

"They've come. They've found us!" he thought. But it was just another stranger. This bigger world seemed full of them. His chest felt as if it had a huge hole in it that ached.

Most of the time now, he managed not to think of home, his family, or Ghost. It was easier that way. He turned his thoughts back to studying the strange people at the fishery.

"I think those there are the same as those," he tried sorting by clothing styles, soon realizing that was impossible. People on the Great River had bargained and traded back and forth so much that what they wore had more to do with trade opportunities than where they were from. The Plains buckskin style of dress was everywhere, often combined with a traditional skirt or cape of

woven grass, feathers, or a piece of store bought clothing from the Hudson's Bay Company.

Tarak switched to trying to identify groups by their facial features and physical builds.

"The short, stocky people with the flattened foreheads are the Chinook," the Numa guard informed him. "Chinook women with babies are easy to spot. They are the ones with cedar planks strapped to their baby's heads. It makes their forehead's grow flat."

"Why?" Yumis wrinkled his nose.

"To honor their gods." The Numa shrugged.

"Will the white giant come here?" Tarak asked, thinking about Jimmy Buckeye's stories.

"Hyas Tee? He lives downriver, at the fort."

"Have you seen him yourself?"

The young man glanced up the bank and sniffed, as if he smelled something worse than the acres of freshly gutted fish drying in the sun.

"Since the missionaries and priests came to the Great River, you do not have to go to Fort Vancouver to see a white man."

Buyers began to gather, looking the slaves over. Some approached the Snake leader, gesturing and asking questions in the Jargon; the trade language used along the Great River that was a combination of Russian, French, English, and Chinook.

Tarak looked at his fellow captives. They had shared a long journey and many trials. Now

CHAPTER 10

they would be split up and sold, each going to their own fate with no witness to what became of them.

"I hope the same person buys us both," Yumis said, nervously.

"Kloshe ko ko stick." Big Woman smiled at them. It was a Jargon phrase that Tarak did not really understand-- something about knocking on wood for good luck.

"Kloshe ko ko stick," Tarak repeated, but he did not believe he knew much about good luck.

CHAPTER ELEVEN

Loo-ee, Jimmy and Ghost approached a tent, one among a city of tents set up on the bluff above Silyalo Falls.

"Ah, Loo-ee, ya' filthy, French devil." A red-haired Scotsman tossed back the flap of his tent and straightened to his full height. "I wondered when I'd be seein' your ugly mug."

Ghost stopped beside Jimmy waiting patiently. Pulling the travois was hard work and though much of his strength had returned, he was not a young pup anymore. His bones ached and his feet were calloused and sore.

"Eet eez good to see you too, Angus." Loo-ee clapped the highlander on the back. "We went south looking for some place zat's not crawling weeth red-headed Scots. But it eezz good to be back, mon amis."

"What is this? A new partner, Jimmy?" The Scotsman eyed the large white dog strapped to the travois.

"This is Skookum. He works cheap." Jimmy grinned. "What brings you upriver, Angus?"

"Kamiakin is selling a herd of Nez Perce horses to Hyas Tee, and I told him I'd help him

CHAPTER 11

take 'em downriver to the Fort. Hyas Tee is buying the lot and happy to get 'em too. They are a fine bunch of beasties, all fire and kick."

"The Nez Perce breed beautiful animals." Jimmy patted Ghost's head absently.

"Anything would be better than the worm ridden swaybacks the Company sends from England." Angus rolled his eyes. "But in truth, I could'na wait to get away from that cold, rainy bluff. The Fort is ankle deep in mud already." He looked around at the wide, open grasslands. "I would'na want to camp at Silaylo during the summer, it bein' the devil's own furnace then, but in September, a body can warm their bones nicely here." He smiled broadly, breathing in the dry air and patting his chest. Jimmy began to unharness Ghost from the travois. "'Tis a fine kamook, Jimmy." The Scotsman nodded at the dog appreciatively.

"You should have seen him when we found him in the mountains." Jimmy shook his head. "He was at death's own doorstep. Isn't that right, Loo-ee?"

"Oui," Loo-ee agreed. "Jimmy he nursed heem and fattened heem up like he was heez own mama."

"He's a tough one. Worth his weight in gold, he is," Jimmy bragged.

"I can see that." Angus McDonald reached out to pet the dog's head. Ghost growled.

"No, Skookum, Angus is a friend. He's friendly once he gets to know you," Jimmy apologized.

The Scotsman withdrew his hand. "I don't hold it agin' him. 'Tis na' a bad thing to be cautious these days. Well, you lads better come inside and have a sit so you can practice all the lies you'll be tellin' downriver at the fort"

Jimmy dropped the travois' harness by the side of the tent and slipped a rope over Ghost's head, tethering him to a peg.

"Rest a bit, Skooks." He ruffled the dog's fur. "I'll bring you something to gnaw on later."

Ghost had pulled the travois for weeks now. Though the wound in his side had healed, an ugly, pink, scar made a deep line through the thick fur and he still favored his front leg. The men had been good company, letting him sit with them by the fire and having him curl up beside them when they slept. They called him Skookum and he answered to that name, but in the early hours of the morning when he was still half asleep, he remembered swimming in a rippling river beneath a snow peaked mountain beside a boy with long black hair and a heart that beat in rhythm with his own. When Ghost woke from these dreams he felt as if he had lost something and couldn't quite remember what it was. An emptiness and longing haunted him and it stretched his spirit thin. He lay down with his head on his paws, letting out a long doggy sigh and dozed.

CHAPTER 11

Somewhere in the camp a boy laughed, the sound tumbling over the tops of the tents and teepees. Ghost raised his head, searching for a half forgotten face, but the laugh faded, lost beneath the rumble of Silaylo Falls and he lay back down, slipping back into his dreams.

CHAPTER TWELVE

A stocky Chinook man and his wife gave the Snake leader a pack horse, an iron pot, a metal digging stick, five blankets, and three strings of dentalia shells in trade for a slave.

The Snake pushed Ti'caw toward them.

"Mamook klatawa: go with them. Klootchman laplash opoots. You too." He pointed at Big Woman.

Big Woman looked him straight in the eyes and did not move.

All the captives became very quiet, waiting to see what would happen.

Tension between the Snake leader and Big Woman had been building since the day he had left Chiwa'chni by the trail. Now she had the chance to make him lose face, maybe even make him lose this sale. Her lips curled up into a triumphant smile as the Snake's fingers curled into fists. Both looked into the other's eyes. Neither flinched.

Slowly, Big Woman slipped her hand under the rope around her waist, holding it out toward the Snake. For a moment, Tarak thought the Snake Leader would cut the slave woman instead of the rope, but the man glanced between the pile of goods at the couple who had bought her. Revenge

CHAPTER 12

could cost him all they had traded for her. Clenching his jaw, the Snake cut through the rope that bound Big Woman to the others.

"I will not be a slave forever," she hissed. "But you will always be a snake. Come Ti'caw." She swayed down the beach like a she-bear, dwarfing her new masters. Ti'caw followed as if caught up in her wake.

One by one the captives were cut off the human string that had bound their lives together and were led away. Tarak felt like a tree having its insides eaten out in tiny little bites by bugs.

Somewhere across the camp a dog barked. It sounded like Ghost's bark but that life was gone now. Tarak shut his eyes.

A group of white men had gathered on the bank above the slave traders. Their faces, unlike Loo-ee Barbo's, were smooth with no lip fur. Most had brown hair like the shades of deer hides. A few had hair the golden color of late summer grass. They did not wear the clothes of a trapper. Their narrow leggings were dark without any decoration and over their chests they wore snow white shirts with shiny shells in a line up the middle.

A tall, thin, Klale man, his skin almost as black as a crows, appeared beside a woman who was his opposite; small and pale. Her clothes covered her from neck to toe. Even her hands were covered and her skirt was wide and full, like an overhanging willow. The only skin that showed was her face, and it was the color of the inside of an oyster's shell, soft and pinkish. The face of the baby in her arms was even lighter and Tarak finally understood why these people were called "white".

"Missionaries," the young Numa guard sniffed, noting what had caught Tarak's attention.

A half dozen village children flowed toward the white woman like a school of brown minnows. Their mothers looked up to see where their children were going then went back to splitting and gutting fish. The mission woman was not a stranger. She smiled warmly as she greeted the naked, sun-browned children by name. A miniature version of the white men jumped out from behind the woman's skirt to join in the children's play. The Klale man looked on in dignified silence as the children, brown and white, naked and clothed, chased around them.

A large group of Natives were gathering below the bluff, to hear a short, thickset man speak. Tarak heard the name "Smohalla" and he could see by the way people listened that the speaker was respected on the Great River.

"Tseepie!" a man's voice shouted from the bluff. "Tseepie!" The young missionary, who had been standing on the other side of the woman, pushed through the crowd, planting himself in front of the Snake Leader. "You take the bad road, brother," he said, his pale face flushed with emotion. "These are your own brothers and sisters that you sell. It is cultus; bad."

CHAPTER 12

The Snake Leader turned his back as if the missionary was not even there.

"Huy huy tillikum, buying and selling people, makes your heart cultus." He pointed to Tarak and the other unsold slaves. "I beg you; have mercy on these poor souls. Do not do this."

The Snake kept staring at the far riverbank. On the bluff behind him the other white men fingered their rifles, nervously. There were many Native people at the fishery and only a few whites but the whites had the pish stick rifles and the Natives did not. If trouble broke out, many innocent people would die.

The mission woman touched the Klale man's arm, glancing at the children and a group of elders sitting nearby. Trouble would be no good for anyone. The Klale man headed down the path.

"Be careful, Winslow," she called after him, motioning the other white men with their rifles to follow.

"Reverend Perkins," the Klale man said, as he approached the young missionary. "You know we all agree that slavery is a terrible curse. I have cause to know better than most, but this is not the time or place. There are women, children and old folks here."

"We should go, Brother Perkins," one of the white men added, putting a hand on the young reverend's arm and gently pulling him away. "There could be trouble if we stay." Together, he and his friends urged Reverend Perkins back up the trail onto the bluff.

"Klahowyum!" Reverend Perkins shouted back over his shoulder.

The Snake spun around. "For us, slaves are like your dolla'. If I don't trade, my wife and tenas tillikum starve to death this winter. When the white missionary feeds my family then I will stop trading slaves," he shouted in jargon.

"It is against the laws of the Sagali Tyee, the Great Chief Above All, to buy and sell souls. You take tillikum's lives and kill their spirits." The white men pulled their passionate friend away from the bluff in a cloud of brown dust.

Tarak's eyes caught and held the gaze of the mission woman.

"Help me," he pled, silently.

With sad eyes she turned away.

The Klale man lingered, the last to go.

People shook their heads and frowned. There was nothing to be gained from such a growl. Neither side had convinced the other of anything.

A shadow fell across Tarak. He turned and looked up. A strange man towered over him. Tall for a Chinook, the man had the flattened forehead of his people, his curved, beak-like nose making him look like a bird of prey. His fine buckskin clothing showed he was a man of wealth. His arms were tattooed with the trade length of dentalia strings and many strings were wound between the marks.

CHAPTER 12

"Go with this man," the young Numa told Tarak. "He has bought you. He is your master now."

CHAPTER THIRTEEN

"We'll take our furs down river to the fort as soon as there's room on one of the le boats," Jimmy raised his voice above the roar of the falls. Jimmy, Ghost, Loo-ee and Angus stood on the cliff above the beach where trade goods were loaded and unloaded from the huge canoes called "le boats." On the beach below, a group of Chinook and their slaves were loading bundles into a large canoe. The slave girl caught Ghost's attention. Where had he seen her before? Something tapped at his brain, as if the memory was an egg inside his head and cracking it open would free what he had fogotten. A boy near the girl spoke and, like a dam his memories flooded back. It was Tarak!

Ghost let out an urgent, joyful bark, pulling against the rope that held him.

"Hush, Skookum." Jimmy said, abscntmindedly, his focus on talking with the other trapper's.

Ghost's feet danced in place and he barked again, quivering with excitement, but Tarak did not look up to the cliff. Instead, he got into the canoe. He was going to leave. He was going to leave without Ghost. The big dog barked and barked and

CHAPTER 13

barked again, the energy of each bark shaking him from the tips of his ears to the tip of his tail.

"Quiet, Skookum! What's gotten into you?" Jimmy pulled the dog away from the edge of the upper bank as the group headed back toward the encampment.

*****

Their new Chinook masters watched Tarak, Big Woman and Ti'caw load the canoe then settle themselves inside as well, waiting for their masters to finish their business.

Suddenly, Tarak stood and looked around, scanning the beach.

"What is the matter, boy?" Big Woman asked.

"I heard a dog bark."

"There are always dogs barking. That's what they do."

"No, this one sounded like my dog, Ghost."

Big Woman shook her head. "Sit down before you tip the canoe over and your new master whips you, boy."

Tarak shaded his eyes, searching the cliff above them.

"He's a big, white dog with ears that stand up like tepees, a black nose, and a bushy tail and eyebrows." Ti'caw looked up at the cliff above them. "You heard him, didn't you Ti'caw?

"I didn't hear anything," the girl snapped, looking away quickly. "A dog barked. So what? It doesn't mean anything. Don't be stupid, Tarak. It couldn't be Ghost this far away."

"It could," Tarak insisted, still searching the cliff.

"How would he get here alone? How would he find you?" She flipped her hair back over her shoulder. "The Snake shot him, Tarak. You saw it. You should face the truth; Ghost is as dead as Chiwa'chni." Ti'caw turned away.

Tarak's jaw clenched. It was a mean thing to say, and she knew it. Tarak's happiness leaked away like water from a hole in a jug.

They were probably right, he thought. If Ghost was alive, he was in the mountains below Wai-i-ka, not at Silaylo Falls, and wasn't that what Tarak wanted, for his friend to be safe where people loved him and would take care of him?

Big Woman looked from Ti'caw to Tarak and shrugged.

"It was just a dog. They all sound alike."

Tarak sat back down, all the hope squeezed from his heart.

The Chinook who manned the paddles pushed the canoe out into the water and it shot forward, heading downriver.

On the cliff above, a large white dog appeared, trailing a rope. Planting his feet, he barked at the boy in the canoe. But the boy did not hear him.

CHAPTER 13

"Skookum, come back! Skooks!" Jimmy Buckeye's shouts rose from behind the dog.

Ghost looked over his shoulder toward Jimmy then back out at the boy in the canoe and began to run downriver.

CHAPTER FOURTEEN

Running felt good. The air whistled past Ghost's ears as his paws clenched the sun warmed dirt. Kicking it out behind him, he flew over the ground. It had been months since he had been able to run just for the joy of it. The hard, plodding routine of pulling the trapper's furs had made him stronger but it had eaten away at his happy nature. The freedom of running again, shucked those days from his shoulders like corn husks.

The white dog raced along the river path, weaving between boulders and trees, rising to high points on the cliffs and dipping back down to the low banks. Sometimes Ghost lost sight of the big canoe, only to find it again when the path brought him to high ground where he could see far out over the water. But as strong and as fast as he was, he could not outrace the Great River and as the sun set; he stood on the ledge of a high bank and watched the canoe disappear over the horizon.

His head sinking low with the setting sun, Ghost limped along in the twilight, continuing downriver.

Before nightfall, he smelled the cook fires of a village. Inland, the dense underbrush of the forest made travel a dark tangle of dangers. Rivers

CHAPTER 13

and canoes were the common modes of travel, so villages clung to their banks. Chinook, Salishan, Klickitat, Yakama. Each village was a family group, not answerable to anyone else. Men, who were recognized for their wisdom, courage, or wealth, became respected elders, but other than giving their advice, they had no control over anyone's actions. There were no kings among the Tillikum.

Ghost skirted the edges of the village, making his way to a rock outcropping where he could see down into it without being seen. Canoes had been pulled up on the beach but he did not see the one he was looking for. There was neither scent, nor sign, of Tarak. Ignoring the rumble in his belly, he turned away, traveling on. His boy was going somewhere. When Tarak got there, he would leave his scent on the riverbank, and Ghost would find him.

CHAPTER FIFTEEN

Hollowed from a single tree, the Chinook canoe was large enough to hold twenty men. Even heavily loaded, it glided across the water as light as a leaf. Tarak slid his finger along the gouge marks on its inner wall. It had been made by the same slow burning and scraping as Kari'wa's dugout; and yet it was a thing of beauty and artistry.

He looked down at the water, watching the current speed them along and understood the strength of this river. It was a powerful being--not small and friendly like the river he knew back home.

The roar of Silaylo Falls fell behind and a silence as large as the wide river itself took its place. Water dripped from the canoe's paddles, birds called to each other, and somewhere in the distance far behind them a dog barked.

"It is just a village dog," Tarak told himself, keeping his face turned downriver.

Big Woman sat with Ti'caw pressed tight against her side. The regal slave woman surveyed the country as if she were a chieftain's daughter looking over her ancestral lands. Tarak smiled to himself. There was no fear in her. She was as

CHAPTER 15

curious about this new world as she would have been if she had chosen to come.

The banks of the river gorge rose higher and higher until they blocked out everything but their own rocky faces. Villages appeared, half hidden by trees, ferns, and bushes, smoke announcing them long before they came into view, but the farther west they traveled along the river, the more often the villages were empty, their roofs falling in, their walls rotting. Scaffolds, holding the dead up to the sky began to line the riverbanks, torn fringe and ragged feathers fluttering in the breeze. Tarak's stomach knotted. What had happened? Where had the people gone?

"Iktah?" he pointed to a deserted village, asking one of the oarsmen to explain.

The man glanced back at the hook-nosed Chinook who had bought Tarak. The stern man sat in the center of the canoe, straight and unbending. He had not spoken to anyone since they left Silaylo Falls and no one had spoken to him.

"White man's sickness," the oarsman whispered to Tarak. "It killed them; all of them. Kumptus?"

Tarak looked away. Yes, he understood. The people who had lived in the villages had not left. They had died. He thought of his own small village high in the mountains, so far away. His people were not rich like the Chinook and the others he had seen here. They did not have the opportunities to trade like these people did, but maybe that was not such a bad thing. The Tillikum had paid a high price for their store-bought clothes, iron pots and strings of dentalia.

The character of the Great River ranged from smooth and glassy to swift and choppy, with stretches of small and great rapids. Twice, the slaves had to unload the canoe so the oarsmen could portage around whitewater too dangerous to navigate. The ten oarsmen carried the canoe above their heads, while the slaves hauled their master's goods along the river path. When the water grew calm again, everything was loaded back in, and they continued on.

As the sun set, clouds of mosquitoes swarmed over the water. The Chinook masters retreated inside their fine wool trade blankets, leaving their slaves, and the oarsmen, to the merciless insects.

Twilight deepened to darkness and a large, rocky island appeared in the river. There were no sounds of life, and no glow or smoke from cook fires. Tarak prepared himself for the sad sight of another dead village but as the current swept them closer to the island, he could see a lone man, standing on the eastern cliff, leaning on a staff. Tarak's skin tingled like centipedes were fidgeting across it.

"Iktah? What is that?" he asked the oarsman, pointing to the island.

The man kept his face turned away. "Memeloose," he whispered. "The home of the

CHAPTER 15

dead. Siwash Bone Turner", he gave Tarak the lone man's name, his voice raspy with fear and superstition.

The Bone Turner's voice carried across the water but Tarak could not see who he was talking to. The strange little man seemed to be the only one on the island.

"Wawa siwash?" Tarak asked the oarsman.

"Naika wawa memeloose. The Bone Turner speaks to the dead." The oarsman held his hand up to his eyes and looked at the Bone Turner through the splayed fingers, motioning Tarak to do the same. "Don't look at him straight on. It is cultus; bad. He has powerful tamanawas."

Tarak held his hand to his eyes and studied the island as they floated by. There was a beach where canoes might land, and inland, behind a fringe of cottonwood trees, he could see a rough plank roofed building.

"There is a village there?"

The bowman bugged his eyes and shook his head. "No. Memeloose, cultus. Only the dead live there--the dead and their keeper, the Bone Turner. Skookum tamanawas; strong spirits," he muttered.

"Skookum? What does it mean, skookum?" Tarak asked.

"Skookum." The oarsman acted out a man dying and the spirit that he became afterward.

"Skookum; it means ghost." Tarak closed his eyes and clamped down hard to stop the thoughts that struck at his heart. *"Don't think about*

Ghost. Don't think... I am stone and stones do not cry," he told himself.

"Yahka lemolo." The oarsman imitated the face of a crazy man, pointing to the Bone Turner. "Powerful tamanawas but lemolo. Kumptus?"

"Lemolo; crazy." Tarak nodded. If the Bone Turner lived alone with only dead people to talk to, it was not hard to understand why he was lemolo.

Big Woman muttered a prayer of protection.

The moon was high by the time the canoe arrived at Gulasquo village. Set under the shade of a grove of cottonwoods, golden firelight winked from the doors of the lodges. The night was still warm enough that people moved around visiting-- shadowy outlines blinking in and out of the firelight's glow. Tarak felt a wave of homesickness roll over him. Was his family safe? Were they well? Would he ever see them again? He remembered the promise he had made himself, that somehow he would find a way to get back, but it seemed like a boy's foolish wish now.

"Mahash lolo; haul," his hook-nosed master commanded.

Ti'caw and Big Woman hefted their bundles, following the small man and his round wife. Big Woman's load balanced easily on her hip while Ti'caw struggled to carry hers but Big Woman was not allowed to help her. At the edge of the beach the round Chinook woman pushed

CHAPTER 15

Ti'caw toward a path that led around the outside of the village. A herd of ragged children, the older ones carrying the younger ones, paraded after a haggard woman hurrying down the path. She planted herself in front of Ti'caw.

"Hiyeea. This is what you traded my goods for, sister? I've been cheated!" she declared. "This tenas tillikum is cultus." The round woman ignored her, continuing on her own way. "This lazy siwash will not work. Look at her. Mamook sollecks. No laziness from you, pelton siwash. Nanitch! You mamook hard or you won't eat. Kumptus?" The woman struck Ti'caw on the ear. The girl staggered, dropping her bundles. "Mahish. Let that be a lesson to you. Mahash lolo, siwash." The woman spat on the ground, turned and marched back to her lodge, leaving Ti'caw standing alone in the darkness.

Tarak knew Ti'caw to be a difficult person but she had not even said a word. What would happen when she opened her mouth and her stubbornness spilled out?

"Mahash lolo," His master barked at Tarak again, signaling him to follow.

His hook-nosed master's lodge was large and well furnished with piles of furs and blankets spread over platforms for sleeping. Four women in fine buckskin dresses worked by the cook fire. The one directing the others had the flattened forehead of a Chinook with deep-set eyes, ringed by dark circles. Another woman sat by the fire huddled in a blanket even though the room was warm. Her hair was white and her skin very wrinkled.

"Tuck-na-wit," the hook-nosed man called out.

A chubby-cheeked boy stepped from the wooden platform that went all along the lodge's inner walls. He was near Tarak's age, shorter and stockier, with a flattened forehead. His buckskin shirt and leggings were heavily fringed and decorated with shells, his moccasins well made with rich and colorful beadwork. His jet black hair fell loose around his shoulders and a small, round disk of abalone shell pierced his nose. Everything about him said that his was an easy life of privilege. His face brightened at his father's call.

"Tuck-na-wit, potlatch naika." The father poked Tarak's chest. "I give him to you. This slave is yours." He gestured so Tarak would understand. "Tum tum kloshe. So you forget your sadness and live again. Your brother is gone. This slave will keep you company."

"Siniuse, what news from up river?" Men of the village began arriving for a smoke. Without another thought for his son, the hook-nosed father turned and walked away. His son's face fell, and Tarak could see how the boy struggled with disappointment at his father's casual dismissal. He turned and studied Tarak.

"Wawa? You speak Jargon?" He copied his father's stern frown. It looked silly on his round, babyish face.

CHAPTER 15

"Tenas; a little," Tarak answered.

"Kloshe." Tuck-na-wit poked Tarak's chest. "No kahpo wake. You are not my brother. Kumptus? You are kapoots sill; a rear end saddle, eh?" The boy jabbed his thumb at his own chest. "Tuck-na-wit is hyas muckamuck here." He circled Tarak, looking him over as if Tarak were a horse he was thinking about buying. "I will call you Boy."

Tarak shook his head, putting his hand on his chest. "Tarak."

Tuck-na-wit's lower lip stuck out beyond his receding chin line. "'Boy'," he insisted, plopping his butt down on the edge of the wooden platform. "Boy, I am thirsty. Mamook chuck. Bring me water," he commanded. "Chako!"

Tarak looked around. A tightly woven bag hung from a peg near the doorway. He started toward it.

"No." Tuck-na-wit stopped him. "Ticky; you get me fresh water." He picked up a smaller, empty water gourd from the platform and tossed it at Tarak's feet. "Lolo hyas chuck." He pointed towards the river, his eyes daring Tarak to disobey. "And don't get it from where they bring in the canoes, it's always muddy there. And don't get it from where the women wash either. The babies always pee there." Tarak did not move. "You are a stupid siwash. You don't know anything, do you? I hope my father did not pay much dolla' for you." A mean smile twitched at the corners of Tuck-na-wit's mouth. It was not his father's tight-lined mouth yet, but it might learn to be.

Tarak's cheeks burned with anger and shame. He had just gotten here, how was he supposed to know where the women washed and the babies peed? *I am stone. I am stone*, he repeated to himself. A stone would not care if no one noticed it was tired or hungry, or if they were mean for no good reason. He carried the gourd past the circle of men smoking their pipes. They did not even look up to see him. He was invisible to them, a non person, a slave.

Outside the lodge, Tarak looked up stream then down. The paths curved gently, following the terrain; much like they did in his own village. Things could not be so different here. People would wash and bathe downstream so the water would be clean upstream. There would be paths leading to the places people used. All he had to do was find them.

As Tarak neared the shore, the bushes ahead rustled. He froze, a cold worm of fear crawling up his spine as a low gravelly voice began to chant. Tarak did not understand the words but he could feel the power moving. This was magic.

"Axe' ki", he thought with a shiver, trying to see between the branches of the bushes.

The demon wore a badger skin on its head, the animal's body trailing down his back, a claw necklace circling its neck. Its arms rose, holding a single hair up to the moonlight. They were banded

CHAPTER 15

by strips of badger pelt but they were a man's arms. The man crouched down, getting closer to his work.

Tarak leaned forward, his curiosity spiced by fear.

A dozen small, white points, like an open mouth of sharp teeth made a bright circle against the dark ground. The man placed the hair in the center as he chanted.

"Elann Konaway Se'ah host. Ticky, ticky, mahook. Mamook huy huy, Se'ah host. Iksum skookum, Sagali Tyee. Hyas muckamuck chako skookum. Chako oleman. Konaway kokshut, Se'ah host. Mahish. Mahish…

The hair on Tarak's neck stood up. People were careful to burn any loose hair or fingernails, knowing they were highly prized by magicians for casting spells against their enemies. Someone had been careless and now they would pay for it.

A twig snapped nearby and the chanting stopped.

Tarak breathed slowly through his nose as his father had taught him to do when he hunted, hoping he would not be discovered, but suddenly strange words were sucking at his ear, the breath of them hot and foul. Hands moved to encircle his neck.

Tarak struggled to remember the Jargon words that could explain who he was and what he was doing here.

"I was just fetching water." He held up the water jug, speaking in his own language. "I was getting water." Tarak remembered the words Tuck-na-wit had used. "Mamook chuck. Tuck-na-wit mamook chuck."

The hands disappeared from his neck and a throaty voice laughed.

"Cheechako; you're new." The man's teeth were half gone and those he had left were so rotten they made his breath stink like a skunk.

"Mamook chuck." Tarak held up the water gourd.

"Mamook chuck. Alta!" The badger man melted into the trees.

Tarak took a few deep breaths. Shadows dripped darkness onto the path but there was nothing he could do but go on. If he returned empty handed, his boy master would know he had been afraid and never let him live it down. Cautiously, Tarak made his way to the water and filled the gourd. He was headed back when he almost tripped over something in the trail.

Ti'caw jumped up, her face streaked with dirt and tears.

"Watch where you're going, you stupid boy," she stomped off.

Tarak was not the only one learning what it was to be a slave tonight.

CHAPTER SIXTEEN

The trappers had not been cruel masters but his life with them had been centered around the burden of heavy work, with no room for play. There had been no wading in the water just because it sparkled, or napping in the sun for no other reason but that it felt good, and now Ghost again took time to enjoy being a dog, with doggy curiosity, playfulness, and frequent napping. But, the nameless longing had a face again and though he took time to chase squirrels, nothing would keep Tarak and him apart.

The ground shook, waking Ghost from a deep sleep. He jumped to his feet. Where was he? What was happening? The smell of horse sweat and the beat of hooves made him want to hide. Backing up, he crouched under a low bush.

He had been traveling downriver for days, hunting when he was hungry and drinking from the river.

The first horse raced past Ghost, tossing its mane and stamping its feet. Three more followed and soon the trail was clogged with animals snorting and neighing, swishing tails and stamping hooves. Two men rode in, pushing the herd into a tight group.

E.F. WINTERS

Ghost recognized the Scotsman, Angus McDonald, who had been with Jimmy and Loo-ee at Silaylo Falls. The red-haired man circled around the rear of the horses on one side, while a burly Native, with the build of a bear, pressed them on the other side. A third man joined them, bringing in a few stragglers.

Healed and healthy again, Ghost did not need someone to look after him, but once the first thrill of freedom had faded, he found he missed people. He made a small, lonely whimper.

The burly man leaned over and looked under the bush.

"Where did you come from, old kamooks?" He sat back up and scanned the path ahead. "There are no villages for miles."

"Be careful, Kamiakin. Wild dogs can be dangerous," Angus warned him. "It might have a disease."

The man Angus had called Kamiakin chuckled. "You King Georgemen say that about everything. It's wild; it's dangerous; it could have a disease, but since you came, it's us who've been dying."

"I'm no man of King George's," the Scotsman protested, hotly. "I'm a red blooded Scot and wild as any of you lot and don't ya be forgettin' it."

"Ah, that's just wawa, Angus, and wawa is just noisy air."

CHAPTER 16

"At least his noisy air comes out his mouth!" The third man hooted, startling the horses so they trotted forward.

"Chako! Let's go, you devils!" Kamiakin urged his horse on down the trail. "It's still a long way to Fort Vancouver."

It was full dark when Ghost came on the horse trader's camp. The three men had laid out their bedrolls by a fire, eaten and settled the herd. One of the men was already asleep but Angus and Kamiakin drank tea from tin cups. Ghost moved in warily, drawn by the familiar sights and sounds of camp.

"Is that your friend from the trail?" Angus asked, noticing the dog.

Kamiakin looked up. "That's him."

"I know this dog. He was with Jimmy Buckeye and Loo-ee Barbo, pulling travois. What's he doin' here, all by himself?" The Scotsman pulled out a bit of hardtack from his pack and took a bite. Ghost made no move to come closer. "Well, it is'na a handout he's lookin' for."

"A big dog like that can take care of himself." Ghost lay down. Resting his chin on his paws, he watched the men from beneath bushy white eyebrows, his eyes slowly growing heavier as the firelight made shadows that settled into the lines of Kamiakin's face.

"People talk about a new village Hyas Tee builds for whites at the falls on the Willamette."

Angus nodded. "It's good land and there's plenty of room to grow."

"Now that the fever has killed most of those who lived there before, you mean," Kamiakin muttered.

Angus' jaw tensed. He had heard the stories about villages given disease infected blankets and how the water was rumoured to have been poisoned by whites on their big sailing ships. His own people had suffered for generations at the hands of British invaders and still he could not believe the stories.

"The sickness was a terrible thing for everyone," he said, quietly.

"Not everyone, it seems."

"Everyone," Angus insisted.

"But why does Hyas Tee need more land? The fort and all its lands are not enough?"

"The fort does not belong to McLoughlin, you know that, Kamiakin. It belongs to the Hudson's Bay Company and someday he will leave the Company and when he does, he and Marguerite will need someplace to go."

"Then he should go back home to his own country. All of you should."

"For many of us this is our country now. Our wives and children are your sisters and daughters. Our homes are with them, here on the Great River."

"Take them with you."

CHAPTER 16

"Pearl could never leave her village and her family." The old Scot shook his head. "We can'na take Indian wives and half Indian children back to the old country. They'd never be accepted. They would be miserable there."

Kamiakin seemed lost in thought. When he finally broke the silence, he said, "When I was at my father's village among the Nez Perce, I heard stories about how bad things have gone for the tribes in the East. Many promises were made and many promises were broken. The people suffer."

"This is not the East," Angus pointed out. "Hyas Tee would never break his word to the Tillikum."

"And yet he helps these new people who come to steal our land."

"He has a soft heart. When the rapids at Wye-wye-eke turn their rafts over, they lose everything. He can'na just let women and children starve."

"And what happens when Hyas Tee is not Hyas Tee anymore?"

"He will always be Hyas Tee."

"You said yourself that someday he will leave the Company."

"He will still be Hyas Tee."

"Maybe. Maybe not. When the Company first came to our lands, we did not fight them. We let them hunt and trap, build their fort, and marry our women and it seemed good, but these new settlers are not like you. They do not want to be neighbors or become part of our families. They have no interest in who we are, or how we live. So why do they come, Angus? This is not their place. What do they want here?"

Angus looked up at the fir trees making lacy cutouts against the starry sky. Their scent perfumed the air. Turning his head he could see the Great River glistening like a wide ribbon flowing across the earth and sighed.

"There are trees here that are so big around that four grown men can'na link their arms about them," he told his friend, wistfully. "Sturgeon come out of the water the size of dolphins. You put a seed in the ground here and it sprouts without you doin' enna'thin'; the earth is that rich. You canna' understand, Kamiakin, because all you have ever known is paradise. You've never seen the old world with its stink and disease--the chimneys belchin' smoke all day and night. You canna' understand how the hope of havin' something for the first time in your life drives a man when all he's ever known is the misery of havin' nothin'. The dream of livin' where no man has the right to beat you just because of his family name, where you dinna'have to sit by helpless, watchin' your bairns die or be ground under someone else's heel because they think they're blood makes them better than you, even though you work three times as hard. Most of these men have never had enna'thin' in their whole sorry lives. They see this as a chance

CHAPTER 16

to change all that for their families for generations to come."

Kamiakin shook his head. "The only difference between what they left behind, and what they want to build here is, this time, they plan on being the ones doing the crushing."

Angus' mouth drew into a tight line. How many years did it take to make a place your home? Was just watching your child born there enough? Did it happen because you built a cabin, or planted a tree? The Tillikum had lived on the Great River for more generations that anyone could count, but Angus McDonald loved the land and its people as if he were one of them. He had not thought of himself as an outsider for a long time.

"We have nowhere else to go," he said, finally, pulling his bedroll around him and turning his back to the fire.

Kamiakin took a sip from his cup. The tea was sour and cold. He poured the dregs on the ground. The white dog dozed at the edge of the fire's light. He had not come closer, but he had not left either.

"You have friends upriver, an easy meal, a bed by the fire, and yet you choose to travel alone, old kamooks. I guess you did not like pulling the white man's burdens, eh?"

Ghost had fallen asleep by the fire, but by first light he had moved on. Lonely or not, he had to find his boy.

CHAPTER SEVENTEEN

A heavy mist blanketed Gulasquo village's cedar-plank lodges. A slow dawn warmed the air, threads of mist twining snakelike through the trees, rising to disappear in the emerging blue of the new day.

For Tarak, life among the Chinook was both as strange and familiar as life in any village. People woke up, worked, played, visited, ate, and slept then did it all over again the next day. Being the trade link between the Plains people and their Coastal neighbors, who lived on the edge of the Pacific Ocean, had made the Chinook of the Great River a wealthy people. They had few daily chores themselves. Slaves took care of those things, leaving their masters time to visit, do beadwork, basketry or woodworking. Their skill in these crafts was admired and their work highly prized, for they built beautiful things.

In Siniuse's lodge, slaves outnumbered the family and as the only living son; Tuck-na-wit was given anything he wanted. It had not made him grateful. He was a spoiled, bad tempered boy, whose greatest joy was ordering Tarak around and sending him on pointless errands, just because he could.

CHAPTER 17

Tarak sat up on the sleeping platform that he and Tuck-na-wit shared, awakened by the sounds of the slave woman, Lala, stirring acorn mush in an iron pot over the fire. Climbing out from under the hide bed covers, he rolled off the pine boughs that served as the bed's mattress.

"Good morning, Auntie," Tarak addressed Lala politely. "Breakfast smells good. Tuck-na-wit will be hungry when he wakes."

"When isn't he hungry, that one?" Lala made a grunting sound as she squatted, driving a fart into the ground. Her fat, brown lips rolled into a proud grin.

Lala's farts were the stuff of legend. A slave could not talk back to their master but there was no stopping gas. It came when it came and if it happened to make a point about a non-person's opinion, well, who could prove it?

"He acts like he's a chief already." Lala scraped the mush off the sides of the pot and lowered her voice. "Big Woman was at the river this morning. She told me poor Ne-mamooks died last night. Heah-yah." There were few joys in a slave's life; gossip was Lala's. "In four days when they take Ne-mamooks to Memeloose that skunk-smell of a magician, Se'ahost, better watch out." Lala pursed her lips together.

Tarak cocked his head to one side. "I don't understand, Auntie. What has Ne-mamooks dying got to do with Konaway Se'ahost?"

The slave woman ladled mush into two carved wooden bowls. "Big Woman's mistress told her that someone, she wouldn't say who, saw Se'ahost cast a spell on Ne-mamooks because when Se'ahost first came to Gulasquo, he wanted to marry Ne-mamooks oldest daughter and Ne-mamooks said no." Lala slurped mush from the ladle, rolled it around her mouth then nodded in approval.

Tarak had seen Ne-mamooks' daughter. She was old—-over twenty winters. It was hard to understand someone keeping a growl alive for so long. It was even harder to understand the argument being over a girl. Tarak remembered the first time he had seen Se'ahost in his badger skin headdress with his claw necklace, and the tooth circle ceremony that Tarak had interrupted. For weeks he had waited to be struck down by the tawati's magic, but Se'ahost had no interest in a slave boy.

Lala made a face as if she had bitten into a bitter acorn that had not been soaked long enough.

"Don't be fooled, Tarak. Se'ahost may act lemolo but he is not without tamanawas." She placed carved bone spoons in the bowls then leaned in close to Tarak's ear as she handed the bowls to him. "Big Woman also told me they caught Ti'caw this morning."

Tarak frowned. "Caught her doing what, Auntie?"

CHAPTER 17

"Trying to run away, of course. Didn't you hear?"

"Ti'caw tried to escape?" Tarak was shocked. What was the girl thinking? Did she have any food? Did she even have a knife? Winter was coming. How did she expect to travel all the way home without anything she needed to survive?

Ti'caw was the only slave to a demanding mistress with six terrible children. She was always busy. Everyone in the village knew her owner as a mean-spirited woman, who worked the girl too hard, but no one interfered. It was no one else's business. As much as Tarak hated Tuck-na-wit's bossiness, he knew his new life was much easier than Ti'caws. Ti'caw did not sleep on a platform near the fire under warm hides. She slept on the ground outside her mistress' lodge, wrapped in a ratty, lice infested hide, listening in case one of the children cried in the night. She did not eat warm, acorn mush, fresh from the pot. She scrabbled for scraps like a dog and she was beaten regularly.

"What will they do to her?" Tarak asked.

"Beat her harder, of course. Oh, don't worry, they won't kill her. But if I know Ti'caw's mistress, the girl will wish they had. Be extra careful today, Tarak," Lala warned him. "When one slave causes trouble all the masters get mean."

Knowing what was happening in the village helped slaves keep clear of other people's growls. The trouble was Tarak wasn't sure if this was someone else's growl. Ti'caw would rather spit on him than accept his help but he still felt responsible for her.

Lala watched Tarak's face. "There's nothing you can do for Ti'caw. There's nothing any of us can do. The girl is her own worst enemy. She would do better to let go of that big pride she drags around." Lala sniffed. "Whoever she thought she was before, she needs to learn that now she's a slave, like the rest of us. Until she understands that, they will keep beating her. Maybe you can help me out later, eh?" Lala changed the subject, setting Ti'caw's problems aside like a dish that had grown cold. "Our mistress asked me to prepare a package for the Bone Turner when the canoe takes Nemamooks over to Memeloose. It is time for new clothes and a blanket for Old Grandmother's husband."

Tarak frowned. "I thought Old Grandmother's husband was dead."

"That doesn't mean he doesn't like new things."

Lala was not Chinook but she had been in Siniuse's lodge since Tuck-na-wit's mother came there. Besides all the gossip, she knew all the village customs. She shook her head at Tarak's ignorance.

"Don't your people take care of their dead, Tarak? You must have many angry spirits in your village. Old Grandmother's husband was a mean, old siwash when he was alive. I hate to think how hard to please he is now that he's dead. Heah-ya."

CHAPTER 17

She made a gesture as if warding off the old man's spirit. "The Bone Turner will dress him in his nice new clothes and wrap him up in his new blanket and his spirit will be much happier."

Tarak's face puckered in disgust. "The Bone Turner is going to change a dead man's clothes?"

Lala blinked. "Dead people like new things too. Old Grandmother's husband was an important man. He has a reputation to keep up in the spirit world. The Bone Turner talks to the spirits and cares for the dead. It is a very important position." Her voice dropped to a whisper again. "But the women say that if he touches you, your spirit goes to the other world and is trapped there. So don't let him touch you. I don't know if it's true or not but there's no sense taking chances." She patted his arm.

"Lala, how long has Old Grandmother's husband been dead?"

Lala looked up at the ceiling, thinking. "Six winters."

Tarak looked down at the bowl of mush in his hands. He wasn't hungry anymore.

Tuck-na-wit sat up among the pile of hides, his black hair sticking up like twigs in a bird's nest.

"Boy." He pointed at Tarak. "Is that my breakfast?"

"Tuck-na-wit is calling me, Auntie," Tarak excused himself.

E.F. WINTERS

Lala farted. "Let him call. It will do him good to learn some patience." As she busied herself with filling more bowls of mush, Naha, Tuck-na-wit's sad-eyed mother, entered followed by Siniuse, his hooked nose apple red from the cold.

The wild roses that had been placed around the lodge to protect the family from Tuck-na-wit's dead brother's spirit had been dry so long they were brown sticks, their petals all blown off but Tuck-na-wit's mother had still not shaken off her eldest son's death. Most days she sat with her beadwork forgotten in her lap, staring at nothing. It was Lala who ran the household now.

"Today we will go upriver," Tuck-na-wit announced as he and Tarak headed for the door.

Siniuse looked up from his breakfast. "Stay away from the white men's mission. Tumeocool told Tot the Boston Klauchman's wagons cover the land around it like a flock of hungry birds, picking its bones clean."

Tuck-na-wit's uncle, Tot, grunted agreement as he entered.

"Smohalla says there are so many white men coming that they will cut up the whole earth with their plows. They will fence all the land in so the tillikum will have to grow wings or burrow beneath the ground like gophers to go anywhere except on the river."

Siniuse shook his head as he readied his pipe for a smoke.

CHAPTER 17

"White men would fence the water if the spirit of the river were not so strong."

Many villages had opened their homes to the young missionary, Reverend Perkins. Villagers from up and down the River had been to the mission's revival camp and listened to the young minister preach from the "Book of Directions". Hundreds had been baptized in the new Christian religion and now practiced it alongside their old ways, but not Siniuse. The hook-nosed elder did not like white people, and he did not like anyone else liking them either. Though he was given the respect of an elder, he could not tell others what to think, or do. The tillikum of the Great River made up their own minds about things and the advantages of store-bought clothes, iron pots, and metal knives were hard to argue with. People wanted these new things. Even Naha had them.

"I'll race you!" Tuck-na-wit ran ahead of Tarak.

A dozen canoes were beached at the village landing. One of the men looked up from his bartering with visitors.

"Have you come for another canoe lesson, Tuck-na-wit?" the Gulasquo man asked.

Tuck-na-wit frowned. Having a grown up around telling him what to do was not part of his plan.

"Not yet, Uncle." He answered respectfully, though the man was not a relative. "I still need to practice what you already taught me, first."

Tuck-na-wit and Tarak strained to push a canoe into the river. The man approached, but did not offer to help.

"A smaller canoe is easier for two," he said, casually.

Tuck-na-wit's lower lip stuck out and he pressed his shoulder to the canoe's side, grunting with effort. "I must practice with a real canoe, Uncle. Not a child's toy."

The man shrugged. "You will not be able to portage such a big canoe with only two." He walked back to the others still trading on the beach.

Experience was a good teacher. A child who did not listen to a warning from an elder, learned from their mistake; and remembered the lesson.

Tuck-na-wit stopped pushing the big canoe and stood with his hands on his hips, breathing hard. He eyed the other canoes on the beach.

"I like that one better," he declared, leading Tarak to a smaller canoe. They renewed their efforts, pushing the smaller canoe into the shallows then clambered in and headed upriver. The high pitched cry of a girl in pain came to them across the water.

"Someone's getting a beating." Tuck-na-wit grinned cruelly.

Tarak gripped his paddle so hard the knuckles went white. It sounded like Ti'caw.

CHAPTER EIGHTEEN

The Wascopum mission sat on a swell of land with the Great River stretched before it to the North and a high bluff to its South. A wall of peeled logs was set around it like a row of guards standing shoulder to shoulder. Three hundred acres of land were plowed and ready to plant in grain as soon as spring came, but first would come the long, cold winter. Whatever the Missionaries and the tillikum who worked alongside them had put away from the fall harvest was all they would have now to get them through to spring. With the arrival of the American settlers, who came expecting Christian charity, everyone would be hard pressed this year.

As Tuck-na-wit steered the canoe in toward the Wasco village on the banks below the mission, Tarak could see wagons dotting the land on the bluff above. The people moved like busy ants.

"Where are we going?" Tarak asked.

"I am close to my Uncle Squill's village. I must visit." Tuck-na-wit stuck out his chin.

"Squill was at Gulasquo only the day before yesterday," Tarak pointed out, not adding that Tuck-na-wit had invented an excuse to avoid this unpopular uncle.

E.F. WINTERS

Tuck-na-wit frowned. "That is why I must now visit him at his village. It is our custom--something a slave would not understand."

"Your father said—"

"Who is the slave and who is the master here?" Tuck-na-wit scowled.

Tarak knew the answer. Tuck-na-wit reminded him a hundred times a day. They ran the canoe onto the sandy beach, jumped out, and began hauling it out of the water. When they were done, Tuck-na-wit stood with his hands on his hips surveying the area.

"Squill wawa tenas tillikum. Squill's children go to the mission school," he informed Tarak. "He says his nephew can already make his name in the white man's talking lines."

Tarak shrugged. "Squill says a lot of things." Everyone knew most of them were lies.

Tuck-na-wit puffed out his chest, trying to look big and grown up. He looked ridiculous. "I have decided I will learn the secrets of these talking lines."

"Your father will--"

Tuck-na-wit glared at Tarak. "I will not tell him, and you will not either, or you will be beaten. I will learn in secret. Then when the white men come with their papers and no one in our village knows the magic of the talking lines, I will step forward and say, 'I, Tuck-na-wit have this knowledge.' Then my father will be happy he has a second son."

CHAPTER 18

Tarak snorted. It was pointless to bring up the fact that Siniuse had specifically told Tuck-na-wit not to go to the mission and he would probably not be pleased at all about being disobeyed, but in the weeks since Tuck-na-wit became Tarak's master, Tarak had come to understand that the spoiled boy heard only one voice; his own. Tuck-na-wit was right about one thing though, Tarak wouldn't tell. If Siniuse found out, it wouldn't matter whose idea it had been, Tarak would be the one who was punished. Reluctantly, he followed Tuck-na-wit up the bank.

"Maybe they won't let us go to the school. Maybe we are too young to learn the secrets of the talking lines."

Tuck-na-wit shook his head. "Squill's nephew is younger than me by two winters and he goes. Squill says the school was made for tenas tillikum."

Completely abandoning the pretended 'visit', Tuck-na-wit led Tarak around the edge of the Chinook village to avoid being seen and having his visit reported back to his father. Slave and master climbed the hill to the mission compound.

A dozen men from the Chinook, Clackamas and Klickitat people squatted outside the wooden gates, playing the Hand Game.

Inside the mission walls, everything was straight and square. Squares divided the plants in the garden from everything outside it. They divided one kind of plant from another, the animals from the people. There were square buildings and square yards. The wide paths between the buildings had rows of young trees planted along them in long, straight lines. It was as if the white men expected everything in their world to stand at attention in a line, waiting for orders. This was a very different world.

There were still tillikum, but also white settlers, and round-shouldered men with brown skin and flat faces who dressed like white men but didn't move in the same fast, jerky way. Tarak recognized the klale man he had seen at Silaylo; the man with midnight black skin. *Winslow,* Tarak remembered the mission woman calling him.

Tuck-na-wit pointed his finger. "I will tell the klale man that I want to go to the school." He marched up and addressed Winslow in Jargon.

"Ticky iskum mamook tzum tzum."

Winslow studied Tuck-na-wit. "Wawa Reverend Perkins and Brother Equator." He pointed out the young missionary, talking to a Native man dressed in a white man's long blue coat and trousers.

Tarak was grateful when Tuck-na-wit approached the Ka klasco elder, Equator, with a little more humility than he had shown Winslow. Tuck-na-wit's father often called Equator a fool for believing in the white man's Book of Directions and taking on white ways, but Equator had carved out a place of respect for himself among those who

CHAPTER 18

practiced the new faith and he had no reason to indulge Tuck-na-wit's arrogant ways.

"Please, Uncle Equator, I wish to go to the school," Tuck-na-wit said. "I wish to learn the wawa of the tzum tzum, talking lines."

Equator looked Tuck-na-wit over, raising an eyebrow. "You're Siniuse's boy, yes? Does your papa know you are here?"

Tuck-na-wit bit his lip. "It is to be a surprise."

"Well, it will be that." Equator considered this, alert to the possibilities. Having Siniuse's son attend the school was a little like the Plains people's practice of counting coup on the stoic old Chinook. It might be a small thing but it put a foot in a door that had been closed fast and it might lead to others from Gulasquo coming over to the new ways. Equator turned to the young missionary. "What do you think, Brother Perkins?"

Perkins knew the tillikum's ways and he looked into Tuck-na-wit's eyes and held them so that he could take measure of the boy. Tuck-na-wit did the same.

Perkins held out his hand. "Na sikhs. I'm Brother Perkins."

"Take it firmly," Equator instructed Tuck-na-wit. "It is not a promise of anything. It is just a white man's way to show you are friends."

Tuck-na-wit cautiously took the missionary's hand.

E.F.WINTERS

Releasing Tuck's hand, Perkins held it out to Tarak. Tuck-na-wit slapped Tarak's hand away.

"Yahka no tillikum. He is not a human being." The boy frowned his father's frown. "Yahka keekwullie sakolecks nika. He is underwear. Nika Siwash. My Indian."

Reverend Perkin's eyes became like two stones. "There are no keekwhullie tillikum here--no slaves. Kumptus? And no hyas muckamuck, except Sagalie Tyee, the Great Chief Above All." He pointed to the sky. "Not in my school. Brother Equator, tell Siniuse's boy that either he and his 'friend' come to school as equals or he can go home."

Equator translated the missionary's words into Chinook.

Tuck-na-wit scowled at Tarak as if the whole thing were his fault, but when the men turned and headed toward the school, he followed.

Perkins led them to a one-story building. A dozen children, Native and white, played together outside. The Reverend opened the door and the children jostled with each other to be first to get to their places.

Tuck-na-wit turned to Tarak.

"Mitlite. Wait here until I come back; mamook kalapi," he said in a low voice. "I won't be long. It can't take much time to learn this wawa." He climbed the stairs.

CHAPTER 18

"Kmokst Kahkwa." Reverend Perkins blocked the doorway. "Two equals, or no mamook tzum tzum," he repeated.

Tuck-na-wit's face reddened. The other children stared out at him from inside the schoolhouse. People did not tell Siniuse's son no, and they certainly did not do it in front of others so he would lose face.

"Boy, chako!" Tuck-na-wit called Tarak over his shoulder. As Tarak approached, Reverend Perkins stepped out of the way. Tuck-na-wit stomped inside. Cautious and uncertain, Tarak stepped into the schoolhouse. The young Reverend might be able to force Tuck-na-wit to let his slave into the school, but he had no power over what Tuck-na-wit did once they left. When there was no one around to protect him, Tarak would pay for the missionary's stand.

Inside, the children were now subject to the same rules about straight lines. They sat straight-backed, on rows of long benches. Reverend Perkins walked to the front of the room. The wall behind him was smooth and black with white lines drawn on it. The missionary used a cloth to wipe the lines away then took a white stick and began making new ones. The lines were drawn on the black wall like village men drew plans for a hunt in the dust, and just as easily wiped away.

The missionary drew lines and squiggles, giving each a name and sound, and the children repeated them after him. Some of them knew the shapes and sounds and were eager to show off their skills. Others, like Tuck-na-wit and Tarak, were new and did not understand the secret wawa. Still, Reverend Perkins had a kind word and a smile for each effort.

"Tuck-na-wit." The missionary called on his newest student. "Would you like to try writing a letter?"

Tuck-na-wit swaggered to the front of the room, but making the lines did not come easily to him. Twice the short white stick slipped from his stubby fingers. When he finished, the figures he drew were shaky and bent, as if they were old and sick.

"Kloshe. It is a good beginning." Reverend Perkins turned to Tarak. "And now Tuck-na-wit's friend."

Tuck-na-wit's mouth pulled into a tight line as Tarak shuffled forward.

"No matter what he says, you are still my slave," Tuck-na-wit hissed as he passed Tarak in the aisle. "And I will beat you whenever I want."

Tarak lifted his chin and straightened his shoulders. Tuck-na-wit could do what he wanted after they left, but right now, in this place, the missionary had said they were equals. He held his head up high.

Reverend Perkins handed Tarak the white stick. Powder came off onto Tarak's fingers where they touched it, soft and fine as the finest dust. It felt cool and smooth like it held a special magic.

CHAPTER 18

"Go ahead," Reverend Perkins encouraged him quietly.

Tarak drew one line straight up like the pine trees he knew back home then added a line like a plank roof across the top, carefully copying the original figure from the board.

"Kloshe." Perkins smiled. "And do you remember what sound this letter makes?"

"Teee." Tarak made a sound of a bird calling.

"Yes. Wawa iktah siwash? What do they call you, young man?"

"Tarak," Tarak replied, defiantly.

"Then this is the first letter of your name in English. You learn well, Tarak."

With a grunt of disgust Tuck-na-wit jumped up from the bench and ran out, pushing the door open so hard it hit the wall behind it.

"Boy, chako maha! We're going," he shouted from outside.

All of the children stared at Tarak.

He fingered the white stick as the door swayed back and forth on its hinges, fanning cold air into the warm room.

"Alta!" Tuck-na-wit called, impatiently.

Tarak looked at the missionary, waiting for him to say that he did not have to go--that he could stay here, that Perkins would help him get back home because there should not be slaves, but Perkins said nothing.

E.F.WINTERS

    Tarak put the white chalk stick down and walked back down the aisle between the benches. He had to go with Tuck-na-wit. There was no other place for him.

CHAPTER NINTEEN

"I have had enough of this school." The canoe hissed across the sand as Tuck-na-wit dragged it down the beach. Tarak made no comment. Flattening his shoulder against the wooden side, he dug his heals into the sand and pushed. "What good is making the tzum tzum lines? They say the lines talk, but the only wawa I heard was that lemolo white man's," Tuck-na-wit continued grumbling. "It is just a dumb game. You don't even win anything. I bet they make it all up, like Squill's stories."

The canoe slid into the water and the boys jumped in.

"Lemolo white men." Tuck-na-wit muttered before wrapping himself in a moody silence.

Tarak didn't mind. Anything was better than Tuck-na-wit's constant complaining. The boy had everything and still he could not find peace within himself. Tarak wondered if Tuck-na-wit had been like this before his brother died or if it was that loss that had made him so bitter.

Siniuse's family never talked about their first son. Among their people, after four days of mourning the names of the dead were not spoken again for fear the spirit would hear and return to haunt them. It was Lala who had explained to Tarak what had happened.

"Tuck-na-wit's brother went to visit his mother's people on the Willamette River and got sick. There is much sickness on the Willamette—sickness no la metsin can cure," the slave woman warned. "Some of the tillikum say the sickness came from a magic tamanawas stick the white men on the big winged canoe put in the river. Others say the chief man on the winged canoe let loose evil spirits from a bottle so the whites could take our homes." She shrugged. "All I know is that Siniuse' eldest son's body was returned to be buried on Memeloose and nothing in this lodge has been the same since."

Tarak had been bought at Silaylo Falls to fill the empty place in Tuck-na-wit's life that had been left by his brother's death.

Watching the high rock cliffs, Tarak's thoughts returned to the wonders of the magic tzum tzum lines. He saw them everywhere. There was an "r" carved into the rock above him. There were lazy "s's" in the ripples of the water and a flock of geese flying overhead made a "v".

Tuck-na-wit is wrong, Tarak thought. *They are not made up. They are a part of the great mystery.* He wanted to learn more.

"Kloshe nanitch!"

Tarak landed stomach to boards in the bottom of the canoe.

CHAPTER 19

"What are you doing? Are you lemolo?" He gripped the sides as he tried to right himself.

Tuck-na-wit shifted his weight from side to side, rocking the canoe.

"Ooo! Ooo! Kloshe nanitch; watch out!"

"Stop," Tarak demanded. "What are you trying to do? Drown us?"

"Are you afraid, slave boy?" Tuck-na-wit grinned cruelly.

"No."

"Yes, you are. You are afraid because you are stupid and don't know anything. You don't even know how to handle a real canoe. A baby Chinook knows more than you."

Tarak clenched his teeth as he retrieved his paddle from the bottom of the boat. He knew Tuck-na-wit was trying to get him mad. He also knew that if he hit his master, he would be severely punished. He held his tongue and scanned the water ahead. The current had picked up.

"There's white water ahead." They were coming up on a section they had portaged around on their way upriver. "We should head to shore." Tarak tried to keep his voice steady and his temper cool.

Tuck-na-wit pushed his paddle straight down into the water making the canoe spin in a slow circle. His lips curled.

"You think you are smart because you fooled that white man into believing you understood his talking lines, but you are just a stupid slave boy. I was born on this river. I know every rock and turn." He poked his thumb at his chest. "I have the skills of a man. Someday I will be a chief among my people but you will never be anything but a slave."

A prickly heat stabbed Tarak in the throat. He had had enough.

"Cultus siwash!" He swung his paddle at Tuck-na-wit's head. The canoe tipped sideways, knocking Tarak off balance and swinging the paddle wide. "You are nothing but a spoiled child." He re-gripped the paddle and changed its direction, slapping it across the water. A wall of wet washed over the Chinook boy. His hair stuck to his cheeks in black pointy lines, like war paint, water dripping from his chin. For a moment he looked shocked then his eyes narrowed into small beads.

"What did you call me?" He launched himself at Tarak. The boys tumbled into the bottom of the canoe, wrestling and punching.

"You're a selfish, fool!" Tarak tried to pull Tuck-na-wit's hands from his hair.

"You can't talk to me like that. I own you." Tuck-na-wit pummeled Tarak's ribs.

"No one owns me," Tarak shouted back. "You think you are the only one who has ever lost someone? Drowning us won't bring back your brother."

Tuck-na-wit's face went red with rage. "Don't you ever talk about my brother!"

CHAPTER 19

"He died and that's sad but you still have the rest of your family, your village, your whole life! I have nothing. Everything I love has been taken from me because of you."

"I told you to stop talking." Tuck-na-wit wrapped his stout legs around Tarak, his hands clutching Tarak's neck.

One of the paddles flipped over into the water, followed by its mate as the current took the canoe into its grip.

"Get off me!" With a burst of strength, Tarak freed himself. Retreating to the front of the canoe, he sat, breathing hard. Tuck-na-wit scooted like a crab to the opposite end gasping as well.

Tuck-na-wit suddenly paled his eyes and mouth making perfect "o"s in his face. His lips were moving but Tarak could not hear anything. The rapids ahead roared like a mountain lion. Tarak turned to look where Tuck-na-wit pointed as the bow of the canoe dipped down and the first wave rose over them.

There was nothing they could do. It was too late. An eddy struck the canoe, turning it sideways.

"Straighten it out!" Tuck-na-wit and Tarak both reached for their paddles then realized they were gone. One paddle floated in the water not far away.

"There!" Tarak leaped to his feet and dove in after it. Grasping the paddle with one hand, he kicked hard to get his arms above the water.

"Catch!" He sent the wooden stick twirling through the air to Tuck-na-wit.

"Get in!" Tuck-na-wit shouted as he thrust the paddle down to try to anchor the canoe in place.

Tarak pulled himself back in over the side. "Straighten it out or we'll sink," he warned.

Tuck-na-wit worked the paddle, braking their motion just enough so the current would pull the bow downstream. Sucked into a swollen channel between two rocks, the canoe lunged forward, leaping and bucking.

Boulders rushed toward them like hump backed bison.

"Hold on!" Tuck-na-wit braced the paddle against his body to keep them off the rocks. With a loud crack the wood splintered, pushing him backward past the stern, over the side and into the water.

"Tuck!" Tarak searched one side of the canoe then the other as it bumped from rock to rock, before being caught in a whirlpool at the bottom of the rapids. Tuck-na-wit's head rose above the water, spluttering and coughing.

"I've got you." Tarak grabbed him beneath the shoulders and pulled him back in. Sprawled in the bottom of the canoe, the boys lay on their backs, catching their breath as the sky spun above them. They looked at each other and began to laugh.

"Are you all right?" Tarak raised his voice above the sound of the churning water.

CHAPTER 19

"Kloshe." Tuck-na-wit spit out a mouthful of water.

"Good then." They took their places fore and aft, braced themselves, and got ready to finish the ride.

"You know you are completely lemolo, don't you?" Tarak grinned.

Tuck-na-wit smiled back. "That is just what my brother used to say. Hold on, we're going over!"

The canoe shot over the falls, turned sideways, and dumped both boys into the river.

Tarak hit a rock then another. The water rolled and tumbled him this way and that until he was not sure which way was up.

"*This is my world,*" the Spirit of the Deep roared. "*My tamanawas is great and I do not suffer fools or arrogant boys to trespass here.*"

Cold, wet fingers shot up Tarak's nose and down his throat. He needed air. His lungs ached for a breath but he knew if he tried it that watery breath would be his last.

The water thinned into a twilight night. Tarak knew the path. He was near his village, the fresh scents of pine, sage, and dinner filled his nose. Iri'wa sat outside her cave and she looked up as he came closer.

"*Where is Ghost?*" she asked him.

Tarak looked around. "*Isn't he here with you?*"

"*No.*"

"Then where is he?" Panic punched Tarak in the gut. "Ghost! Ghost! Where are you?" He spun around, searching the landscape. Far away in the distance he heard his friend barking. Each time he barked it came from further and further away.

"He has gone to find you," Iri'wa said. "You must find him."

"I will," Tarak promised.

Tarak kicked his way toward the dingy green sunlight above him, using all the strength he had. He fought the churning water, pressing back against its insistent push downward.

Tarak's feet touched something solid. He bunched his legs up, shoved off and exploded up into the air. Dripping wet, he coughed as he began slogging his way to shore.

Two large le boats were beached on the riverbank. Beside them a group of trappers in buckskins with rifles strapped across their backs and knives buckled to their legs watched him rise from the river. It was hard to tell which of them were Siwash and which were white men, except for the red sashes that marked the French Canadian "voyageurs". Two of the men wore the wool cloth suits that identified them as either King Georgemen, or "Boston klootchmen".

A tall figure stood holding the bridle of a horse carrying a handsome Native woman, her dark hair pinned up in the European style. Tarak had never seen a woman riding a horse before. She wore a jaunty hat, her velvet skirt spread over the

CHAPTER 19

animal's rump and her black leather boots sported shiny silver buckles. The boy's eyes returned to the big man. His thick, white hair stood out in all directions like a baby eagle's pinfeathers. Dressed in a long black waistcoat, he was at least a hand taller than any of the other men in the group and Tarak could feel his piercing blue eyes focused on him even from a distance.

"One of them lives, Hyas Tee!" A voyageur pointed at Tarak.

"I have t'other one, Doctor McLoughlin!"

Tarak turned to see the bow of a le boat overtaking him from behind. Tuck-na-wit was bent over the side emptying his breakfast into the water.

One of the voyageurs on the bank waded out and half lifted, half dragged Tarak onto the beach.

"I'd say zeese boys haf zee luck we come along, eh?"

"For certain, they are fortunate to be alive," McLoughlin agreed.

"Lucky their hair didn't turn white. They'd look like old men before their time." The men laughed.

McLoughlin ran his fingers through his own white mane. The story along the Great River was that his hair had turned white overnight after a canoe accident on the Great Lakes from which he had been the only survivor.

"They're probably just too young and foolish to be properly scared when they ought to be," someone remarked.

Dr. McLoughlin, The Chief Factor of the Hudson's Bay Company, studied the water logged youth.

"The Columbia is not a river to be taken lightly, boys," he said. "Tenas tillikum tseepie; this is a bad place for children. You are lucky to be alive; iksum wind."

"No isisk. We lost our paddles, Hyas Tee," Tuck-na-wit choked the words out.

The voyageurs laughed. "Did you hear that, Doctor McLoughlin? These young braves tried to shoot the rapids without paddles!"

"Did they try it without a boat, too? Because I don't see one."

"Shame on you men teasing the poor boys," the woman scolded. "Haven't they had a bad enough time?" The silver bells on her horse's bridle, jingled when its head moved. McLoughlin smiled up at his wife, warmly.

"They meant no harm, Marguerite." He turned back to the boys. "Ka tillicum? Where are your people?"

Hope shot through Tarak. This was his chance. Jimmy had said that he and Loo-ee knew Hyas Tee well. Tarak could tell the great man what had happened and Hyas Tee would tell Jimmy and Loo-ee and they would help him get back home to his parents and Ghost.

CHAPTER 19

In a flash Tarak remembered his vision in the water. Ghost was not at home. He was somewhere else; somewhere looking for Tarak.

"Hyas Tee...?" Tarak's voice cracked as he struggled to find the words to tell his story in the Jargon.

"Nika papa, Siniuse. Nika Tuck-na-wit," Tuck-na-wit broke in.

"You are Siniuse's boy?"

"That would be Gulasquo village, Doctor; downstream."

McLoughlin turned back to the boys. It was not only his height that made him a giant. His pale eyes had powerful tamanawas.

"Kloshe nanitch, take care," he cautioned the boys. "Youtle tenas siwash tseepie; proud little men on bad road get knocked down. No chako skookum. No hyas muckamuck: boys with foolish notions don't grow to be men. Kumptus? If you want to grow up, you must be careful not to get in over your head. Take one of the le boats and some men and escort these two home." He gestured for one of the voyageurs to take charge of the boys then turned back to his wife. "Shall we resume our journey, Mrs. McLoughlin?"

Tuck-na-wit and Tarak were bustled off to the le boat. The jingle of Marguerite McLoughlin's bridle and the company's happy laughter fell behind.

*****

E.F. WINTERS

It was dark by the time the rescue party came within sight of Gulasquo village but the voyageur's soft, rhythmic singing had announced their approach long before they beached the le boat.

"Kumptus klatawa; we know the way," Tuck-na-wit tried one more time to be allowed to finish the trip without their escort. He had lost the contents of his stomach but not his cockiness and he knew his father would not be happy at having his son brought home by the white men.

"Hyas Tee mahish. Hyas Tee commanded me, and I do what the Doctor says. So you just mitlite and wait, tenas tillikum," the voyageur replied firmly.

With the evening chill of early autumn in the air most people gathered by their fires at night but this night everyone seemed to have found a reason to be outside. Something unusual was happening and they all wanted to be the first to tell about it. Scraped and bruised, hair and clothes still damp, Tuck–na-wit stuck his chin up in the air and did not look either left or right as he led the trappers through the village to his father's lodge.

Siniuse's mouth was drawn so tight it looked like he had no lips at all. Hard, black eyes took in the white strangers standing beside his son.

"Nah Sikhs, Siniuse." The Voyageur greeted the elder. "Hyas Tee sends you potlatch, a gift; these two tenas tillikum. We pulled them out

CHAPTER 19

of the river. I guess they thought they were fish 'cause they'd been for a swim."

Siniuse looked down his long, beak-like nose, turned and walked away.

Naha stepped forward. "Mahsie," Tuck-na-wit's mother thanked the trappers, graciously.

"You're welcome, madam." The voyageur gave a polite nod and headed his men back to the le boat.

Naha pulled her son into her arms, her dark eyes flooded with tears. "When you did not come home at nightfall, I was afraid I had no sons left in this world."

Tuck-na-wit squirmed. "You worry too much. We were fine, Naha. We were together."

Tuck-na-wit's mother turned to Tarak and smiled. "Yes. That is good. You and Boy come dry off by the fire. I will have Lala get you something warm to eat. You must be very hungry."

Tuck-na-wit turned to Tarak. "His name is not Boy anymore. I have decided to give him a new name. From now on, I will call him Tuck-na-wit's Friend." The smile he gave Tarak offered a new beginning for them both.

CHAPTER TWENTY

"You don't want to touch that, Friend." Tuck-na-wit used a stick to pick up an old dry snakeskin. "Witches live in these. You never want to touch them. It's bad luck." The fragile sheath blew off the stick, falling apart before it brushed the ground.

"Thank you, I won't," Tarak assured him.

In the weeks since Hyas Tee and his men had rescued the boys, the trees along the banks of the gorge had turned from the dusty green of early fall to the vivid rust and gold of late autumn. The sharp nip of frost gave a bite to the air and at night, icy gusts tugged at the sleeping hides the boys bunched around them. Every day more of the forest animals disappeared into their dens to hibernate. Winter was closing in on them all.

Since their adventure in the rapids, Tarak's days were no longer filled with stupid errands. He was always with Tuck-na-wit, doing whatever Tuck-na-wit wanted to do. Although his master now called him "Friend", Tarak was careful. People did not change overnight. There was always a chance something would trigger a return of the old Tuck-na-wit.

They were close in age, Tarak a little older, but Tuck treated his slave like a younger nephew

CHAPTER 20

who knew nothing and whom he needed to teach. He took this role very seriously. With crossed arms, he thrust his nose into the air and frowned like his father, speaking in what he imagined was a voice of authority. He had no idea everyone in the village was laughing at him behind his back.

Tarak wondered if he had looked as ridiculous to others back home when he had tried to act grown up. Grandfather A'cmu had said ceremonies did not make a man. Neither did putting on grown up airs.

"I am getting my man-name at the Winter Ceremony," Tuck-na-wit boasted, his breath making cloud puffs in the cold air. Their feet crunched on a layer of brown leaves, releasing a musty scent into the chilly air.

Tuck-na-wit's hand-me-down moccasins squeezed Tarak's toes and pulled at his heels while the dry grass insulation spilled out over the sloppy sides. No amount of dunking in the river's shallows would make the leather fit but with the weather getting colder, poorly fitted moccasins were better than none at all.

"The Winter Ceremonies are the most important of the whole year," Tuck explained as they walked along. "All the tillikum will come to the camp at Ka'Klasco; the Chinook, the Klickitat, Kikiya... everyone. Families will have many giveaways in honor of sons who are becoming men, but mine will be the best."

Tarak hung his head. Disappointment tasted bitter on his tongue. Becoming a man was Tuck-na-wit's dream now, not his. Slaves were not given such honors, but it was not an easy thing to let go of something that had been so important to you for so long.

"Is something wrong, Friend?" Tuck-na-wit asked.

"No. Of course not." Tarak brought himself back. "I was just thinking about how things are so different here. In my village, a boy does not become a man until he has done a Spirit Quest and then brings home his first deer. When he does that, there is a feast and Iri'wa reveals his grown up name."

"Hwah! We do this!" Tuck-na-wit spun around, walking backward so he could face Tarak. Excitement brightened his flat face. "Spirit Quest: you fast and call on the spirits for four days and you cannot come back until they have spoken to you. Konaway Se'ahost sent me last fall, before you came."

"We go for a day and a night in the winter in the snow," Tarak explained.

Tuck-na-wit frowned. "In the snow? That would be hard."

Tarak shrugged. "It is not easy to be a man."

Tuck-na-wit turned back around, walking beside his friend. "I think one day in winter is as

CHAPTER 20

good as more days in the fall," he decided. "Who is Iri'wa?"

Since they had become friends, Tuck-na-wit not only shared things about the ways of his people, but he had begun to show an interest in Tarak's old life. Tarak was not sure at first how he felt about talking about home, but he found that it eased some of the tightness in his chest. Still, there were things he did not share. He never spoke of Ghost. It was too hard, and he could not risk Tuck-na-wit using something so painful against him later, if things changed back to the way they had been before.

"Iri'wa is a shaman woman who lives in a cave outside our village," Tarak explained. "She is like your tawati; Se'ahost. She has powerful tamanawas."

"A woman?" Tuck-na-wit scrunched up his face. "She must be a witch."

Tarak frowned. "She is not a witch. She is a good woman. She heals us and helps guide the people. Among the Kama'twa, Wise Ones are mostly women. I have been in her cave many times."

"Kweesh." Tuck-na-wit shuddered. "I hate going to Se'ahost's lodge. But a woman tawati? Yours are truly a strange people, Friend."

"What about the Bone Turner's house on Memeloose, would you go there?" Tarak challenged.

E.F.WINTERS

Tuck-na-wit's eyes got very round. "Only the lemolo would go there."

The bushes to their right rustled and a deer walked onto the path. Instinctively, the boys froze.

"I have been thinking about this idea your people have about bringing home a deer," Tuck-na-wit whispered. "I like it. It shows everyone that you can help the family in a grown up way." He eyed the deer. "I think we should go hunting, you and I." Tuck-na-wit grabbed Tarak's arm, sending the deer leaping off into the bushes. "Come on!"

"I do not even have a bow," Tarak protested, following his master.

"You can have my old one. I will use the new one gifted to me at my nephew's birthing. I can't use two. Come on, I'll race you back to the lodge."

Supplies were quickly gathered and the boys set off.

Under the green canopy of the fir trees, the forest floor was a spongy bread pudding of decayed wood, leaves and wet, loamy soil. Ferns, vines, moss and thorny underbrush wove together in a thick tangle. The inland forests were hard country to hunt in and twice the boys lost the trail of their prey. Well past mid-day, they still had not gotten their deer and Tarak could feel Tuck-na-wit's frustration growing. A frustrated hunter was not a successful one. His father had always told him that patience was the first lesson of the hunt.

CHAPTER 20

"It's getting late. Let's go back, Tuck," Tarak suggested. "It doesn't matter if we get a deer today or not. We can hunt again tomorrow."

Tuck-na-wit set his jaw. "We are not finished. We do not have a deer." Tuck-na-wit's stubborn streak had two sides to it: plain bullheadedness that landed him in trouble and the focused determination that helped him be successful when he set his mind to something that was important. The trouble was, he had not learned the difference between the two.

Reaching the top of the ridge, the boys rounded a stand of boulders. A bear stood in their path, its muzzle covered with gore, a deer at its feet. The bear raised its head and looked at the boys. Slowly, they began backing up.

"How many arrows does it take to kill a bear?" Tuck-na-wit whispered.

"I don't know. How many did we bring?"

"I don't know. I didn't count," Tuck's voice cracked. "But I bet it's not enough."

From out of the corner of his eye Tarak caught the bottlebrush tail of a coyote disappearing into a thicket.

Are you finished playing tricks on me, brother Coyote? Tarak asked the spirit-guardian silently. *Because, if you do not help me now, this may be the last chance you get."*

The bear watched the boys backing away then slowly began to follow, its huge body swaying from side to side.

"This is not good," Tarak muttered.

"I think we should run," Tuck-na-wit tried to keep the alarm from his voice.

"If we do, it will chase us and run us down."

"We could climb a tree?"

"So can it."

"Not a small one," Tuck-na-wit insisted.

"If the tree is small, the bear will just pull it over and knock us out of it."

"Well, we have to do something," Tuck-na-wit complained. "We can't just walk backward all the way home with a bear following us."

Tarak grinned. "It would make a good winter story."

"If we live to tell it."

"Maybe they will name you 'Brings Bears Home' at the winter ceremony," Tarak teased his friend.

"More like 'Big Bear's Small Dinner. Tuck chuckled.

Tarak got an idea. "You don't care about this old bow much, do you, Tuck?"

"Right now, I don't care about anything but seeing the tail end of this bear."

"Good." Tarak drew back his arm and threw the bow into air. It sailed over the bear's head and landed in the bushes behind it. When the bear turned to see what had rattled the bush, Tarak shouted, "Run!"

CHAPTER 20

They were halfway down the hill when they heard the bear's heavy paws thudding behind them. Tarak knew that when it got within reach, it would take whichever of them was slowest. He would never be a man. The name he would carry for the rest of his life was the one Tuck-na-wit had given him: 'Friend'. If that was to be his name, he would live up to it, he decided, slowing his pace. He could feel the muscles of his back shrink towards his spine--anticipating the painful scrape of the bear's claws.

Something moved on a rock ledge above them and Tarak looked up. A dusty brown coyote sat watching them from the mouth of a small cave. Its yellow eyes met Tarak's.

"This cave is a good den," it said, glancing over its shoulder into the dark hole. *"Big enough for a coyote or two boys, but too small for a bear."* It cocked its head to one side then jumped off the rock, disappearing into the forest.

"This way." Tarak changed course to scramble up the steep, rock-covered hillside. Tuck-na-wit followed. Frantic, he lost his footing on the loose scree and pitched forward, scrambling up the slope on all fours. Tarak was in the lead again.

"You are as slow as a turtle," he taunted, knowing Tuck-na-wit would never back down from a contest.

"Ha! I'll beat you." Tuck got his feet under him and pushed forward.

Tarak looked back over his shoulder. The bear had not changed its course. It was still focused on Tuck. Tarak calculated Tuck-na-wit's speed against the bears. His friend would not outrace it before he reached the cave.

Without warning the ground began to rumble and shake until the whole forest danced. The bear stopped, stood on its hind legs and sniffed at the air, letting out a roar as a fountain of gray ash exploded from Lawala Clough, the mountain who was said to be a maiden fought over by two suitors who shared the horizon.

The bear blinked, dropped to all fours, and began moving forward again.

What can I do? Tarak bit his lip. Grabbing a stone from the ground, he threw it at the bear as hard as he could. It whizzed past the animal's rump, grazing it just enough so that the bear stopped to look and see what had touched it. Tarak had gained Tuck-na-wit only a few moments, but if he could keep it up, Tuck might have a chance. Tarak scooped up three more stones and threw them, one after the other.

"Go away, you brute," he shouted. "Go away and leave us alone!" The first stone hit the bear's shoulder. The next struck it roundly on the rump. The third hit just under the bear's left eye. The creature roared and threw its bulk at the hillside.

"Stop! What are you doing?" Tuck-na-wit shouted. "You're just making it angrier."

CHAPTER 20

"Keep going." Tarak ran to where the hillside dropped off sharply in a cliff leaving a level pathway above it. Choosing larger rocks, he studied the bear's pace, waiting until it would be just below him, and then let another rock fly.

It hit the bear's ear. The animal stopped and shook its head, looking around at the falling flakes, confused.

"Climb, Tuck-na-wit. Climb!" Tarak shouted, coughing as the air thickened with volcano ash. The bear pawed at the flakes as if they were a swarm of bees stinging its nose. Then dropped back to all fours and sprinted forward.

"There's a cave up there." Tarak pointed.

"I see it." Tuck-na-wit waved his arms in front of him to clear a path through the thickening ash.

Tarak picked up a larger rock and turned back to take aim.

The bear was gone.

Flakes of ash from the volcano fell like snow, coming so hard and fast now that Tarak could not see thirty feet away but he could hear the bear huffing and snorting below. It had not given up. It was still there, hidden behind the curtain of ash. He hurried across the slippery scree toward the coyote's cave then leaned over the edge to search below.

A stinking pit of pink flesh, rimmed with teeth, opened in front of him.

"Roooa!" the bear roared in his face. Tarak raised the rock, to slam down on the bear's head as long curved claws raked across his chest, dragging furrows through the leather and into the skin.

"Ahhh!" he cried out in agony.

There was a swoosh and suddenly an arrow was sticking out of the bear's right eye.

"Woo-hoo!" Tuck-na-wit cheered.

Howling and tossing its head from side to side, the bear swept its huge foreleg in a long arc, blindly striking out at Tarak.

I will die now, Tarak thought, seeing the giant paw moving toward him again, everything suddenly slow and unreal, like a dream. But the blow did not come.

A white blur flew through the air, hit the bear's body with all of its bulk and knocked the bear to the ground. Tangled in a ball with its attacker, the bear roared as white and black fur tumbled down the scree, lost in the flurry of ashes.

Tarak watched the grey flakes flutter down around him, feeling disconnected and strangely calm. The day had been fair with no clouds. It was not cold enough to snow. The flakes made no sense. His head spun and his mind shifted.

Tarak looked down at the four red lines striping his new buckskin shirt. Where had they come from? They did not belong there. White as duck feathers, the row of red stars his mother had painted made a handsome edge. Tarak fingered the long, curved slits across his chest, watching the

CHAPTER 20

blood seep through them and drip down across the white leather. The shirt was ruined and he had not even had his ceremony yet.

"Tarak!" A'ni called.

"You must not call him Tarak now." Iri'wa appeared beside his mother. "You must call him by his new name."

"What is his new name?"

Both women turned to Tarak as if he had the answer. But he did not know.

"What is my new name?"

"Friend, hurry!" Tuck-na-wit's voice cracked the vision and it broke apart.

Tuck-na-wit pulled Tarak through the falling ash toward the coyote's cave. A dog barked out a sharp, urgent warning from the forest below. Tarak looked down over the cliff edge as a breeze parted the gray curtain.

Ghost stood planted, facing the bear, growling and ready to fight.

Tarak's heart leapt back to life. "No, Ghost! Come Ghost!" he shouted, each breath burning like the bear's claws were slicing him open again.

"Stop shouting." Tuck-na-wit pulled Tarak away from the cliff's edge. "What are you trying to do, bring it back?"

"It's Ghost. I need to help him." Tarak struggled to form words and get free. Snarls and growls from the fight below rose up through the gray.

"I have to go back."

"You're lemolo. Get inside. You're not going anywhere." Tuck-na-wit pushed Tarak to his hands and knees, shoving him toward the back of the cave.

Weak and confused, the wounds on his chest burning, Tarak crawled to the back and leaned against the wall, waiting for the world to stop spinning.

Tuck-na-wit looked out at the falling ash.

"Lawalla Clough must be very angry," he said. Lines of blood had dripped from the gashes in Tarak's chest and now smeared the cave floor. "You're hurt bad, Friend. You need help. I'll go as soon as it's safe."

"An arrow in the eye--that was a good shot, Tuck." Tarak's voice was stretched thin by pain.

Tuck-na-wit shrugged. "I had to do something. I couldn't just let him kill you."

Tuck-na-wit's arrow had injured the bear but as Tarak's dazed mind replayed the attack, he knew it had not been the arrow that had saved him. It had been Ghost. Ghost had taken the bear down when it would have struck him again.

"Ghost, where are you?" Tarak's spirit called out to his friend.

"I saw what you did," Tuck-na-wit's voice pulled Tarak back. "Holding back so the bear would go after you instead of me, and throwing those rocks. It was brave. It was stupid, but it was brave. Did you really think rocks were going to stop it?"

CHAPTER 20

Tarak managed a lopsided grin. "It slowed him down."

"It saved my life. You saved my life."

"No. Not me, Ghost," Tarak thought. *"He saved us both."* Was his friend alive? Tarak tried to listen to what was happening below, but his own heartbeat had become so loud that it blocked out everything else. Was the fight over? How long had he and Tuck been in the cave? Hours? Minutes? He did not know. Maybe Ghost had run off and lost the bear in the forest and he would come back and find them. Maybe the bear was dead. Maybe Ghost was.

"Where are you, old friend? Where are you?" Tarak's spirit called out again, and again. His mind whirled, pushing reality away.

Ants with the faces of white men poured down over the cliff walls that sheltered the Kama'twa village. The ant-men had gold stones for eyes, sharp, pointed, iron tools for hands and deep, black holes where their hearts should be. Tarak's father and mother stood bravely in their path.

"Help us," A'ni, begged her son.

"Your people need you, Tarak." Iri'wa's face appeared, growing larger and larger; her eyes glowing like two full moons. "The world is coming and they will not understand. Complete your quest. Bring the fire to feed us--bring us the fire of knowledge." Tarak looked down. Ghost was beside him, smiling his black lipped doggy smile. Tarak smiled back then began to climb up the stars.

CHAPTER TWENTY-ONE

Ghost lay where the bear's final strike had thrown him. Unable to stand, his pink tongue licked the trickle of blood that dribbled over his lips. Hot, sticky lines of red striped his left side where the bear's claws had raked through his fur and into the skin beneath. His nose was split and he was smeared in splotches of brown blood from muzzle to chest. Every bone in his old body hurt.

A cold rain began to fall, wetting the gray ash into sticky globs. Painfully Ghost pulled himself across the ground to a rock overhang sheltered by bushes and slowly, carefully wriggled out a shallow hollow. Lying back down, he let the darkness sweep back over him.

Slipping in and out of a vague consciousness, the old dog was half aware of people coming up the hill past him. He heard their voices and the sound of their feet on the scree as they climbed up to the high cave. He knew when they carried Tarak away, passing so close he could smell his boy's familiar scent, but he could not even whimper loud enough to let them know he was there. He could not move and he could not follow. His body was too heavy a weight.

CHAPTER 21

The voices were there again later when people came back up the mountain to take the dead bear away and still the old dog could not move.

When Ghost woke again, all he heard was the soft shush of rain falling. It dripped from the edge of the rock that hung over his small burrow, sheltering it from the back, soaking into the ground around him. How many days had he been lying here? The pinch in his belly said more than a few. The North wind carried the scent of cook-fires, roasting venison and salmon to his nose.

Tarak! The thought brought Ghost's mind fully awake. On stiff, wobbley legs he struggled to his feet and began to stumble downhill toward the village.

"Get out of here, you mongrel!" The small-eyed woman in the first lodge he came to shouted, throwing a rock at his head. Ghost turned away and it hit him on the shoulder. Yelping in pain, he slunk back into the forest underbrush. The cold was deep inside his bones. The old wound on his side felt tight and achy, and the new wounds he'd gotten fighting the bear made each breath painful, but what was worse than the pain was the weakness. His whole body trembled with it and he could not make it stop. He needed to eat, and rest, and be cared for.

The big white dog looked out from under a pine tree, his head low, watching as a band of dirty children came out of the lodge.

"What is going on, Naha?" the woman's eldest daughter asked.

"Nothing. It was just a stray dog," the mother dismissed their questions, heading off to the village.

"There it is!" one of the children pointed at the tree where Ghost hid. The four older children raced toward the pine tree, shouting and brandishing sticks.

Confused, Ghost bolted, running back into the forest.

"Stop that!" Ti'caw shouted after the children. "What are you doing, you naughty things? Only evil-hearted children would chase an old kamooks."

"It's just a dirty old dog, Ti'caw," the oldest boy argued.

"Don't your elders teach you that a dog is half human?"

The boy narrowed his eyes. "We would chase a strange person away if they weren't from our village too."

"Unless they were a friend," his younger brother added.

"If they were a friend, they wouldn't be a stranger lemolo siwash."

Ti'caw crossed her ams across her thin chest. "How do you know this dog is not a friend?"

The boys looked at each other. "Because we've never seen it before."

CHAPTER 21

"It was probably trying to steal our food," the older girl declared. "We can't let it hang around our lodge. It might steal the baby!"

It could have the baby, Ti'caw thought, anger getting the best of her. *The poor, sick thing probably won't make it through the winter.* She knew it was a terrible thing to think, but she could not help it. She was tired, and hungry, and cold, and she could not remember what it felt like to be anything else. The baby might not be the only one who would not live to see spring. Big Woman tried to sneak Ti'caw food when she could but these days Ti'caw could only eat small bits before she threw it back up.

Why should I care if these nasty children want to chase off some scrawny dog? she asked hersef. It was stupid.

"It's cold out. Go back inside," she ordered. Grumbling, the children obeyed.

Ti'caw scanned the forest for any sign of the old dog.

It's not Ghost, she told herself. *It can't be.* It was stupid to think such childish, hopeful things. She wiped her eyes with the back of a grimy hand and bit her lip against the swell of hope expanding in her heart. It hurt so much.

"Stupid, stupid, stupid," she scolded herself under her breath, taking a second swipe at the tears spilling down her cheeks. "No one is coming for you. No one cares. You might as well be dead already." She went back into the lodge and closed the door flap.

*****

Ghost pushed his nose through the pine needles on the ground and mouthed the wet leaves with his black lips searching for something he could eat. Scenting the faint trail of a squirrel, he followed it to a tree and looked hopefully up into the branches. Asleep in its nest it would be easy prey but even in good health Ghost could not climb a tree.

Rain fell on his upturned face, running in rivulets of rusty red down the sides of his nose and washing away the dried blood from his fight with the bear. He lowered his head and continued to nose his way across the ground. Pushing over a rotting stump he found some bugs and a root and ate them quickly. He drank water from the creek trickling down the hillside then pounced at a bird that lit near him on a low branch. He could not catch it though, and the effort just made everything hurt more.

His stomach was an empty bag, hanging deflated, inside his ribs. The last of his energy was draining away. The wind blew up from the river again bringing the smells of food from the village. Sitting on the hillside above Gulasquo, Ghost looked down at the glow filtering through the hide doors of the lodges and wondered why they had

CHAPTER 21

driven him away? Tarak's face filled his thoughts. Where was his boy?

He did not even hear the man come up behind him. By the time he felt the rope around his neck, it was too late.

The man, dressed in filthy buckskins and torn store-bought clothes, eyed Ghost from the other end of the rope. "You're a big one, aren't you?" His attempt at a broken tooth smile came out a snarl. His voice was slippery and foul as if it had been oiled by many lies. "Come here boy." The man held out a hand.

Ghost growled and backed as far away as the rope would let him.

"Hungry?" The man fumbled through the bag slung over his shoulder and pulled out a piece of dried meat. "Ya' want this, don't'cha?" He held the meat out.

Ghost's mouth watered. He did want it. He was very hungry. More than that, he needed it. The stinky man tore off a tiny piece and tossed it at Ghost's feet. Ghost gobbled it down before he could taste it.

"There's more." The man threw another piece and Ghost ate that too, but the man made him take a step closer to get the third piece and the pieces were so small they only whetted his hunger. "Here." The man broke off a larger piece. He offered it but did not throw or drop it. "Come for it."

Ghost did not want the man to touch him, but he wanted the meat. Cautiously, he stepped forward, ready to jump away the second he had the meat in his teeth. Another rope flew through the air and fell around Ghost's neck. A second man stepped out from the bushes.

"You're mine, old kamooks," the first man wheezed.

Ghost did not want to go with the men. He pulled and tugged running back and forth, only to be yanked back into place between the men, held tight by their ropes.

"Stop fightin', you white devil." A heavy fist punched the claw marks on Ghost's shoulder. With a yelp of pain he collapsed.

"What do you want with this flea bitten old thing, Rufus?" The second man eyed the unconscious dog.

"You got no vision, MacPhearson. Someone down at the Fort might just want a big dog like this, once he's been fattened up a bit. A little dog's not good for much but eatin', but a big 'un can carry a heavy load, guard your goods, keep watch for you and scare off folks who would do you ill." He smirked.

"What do you think you'll get for him?"

"Something, and that's more than the nothing we got now. Put that bag over his head and let's get him down to the canoe."

*****

CHAPTER 21

Stepping through the doorway, Ti'caw saw two men carrying something heavy in a burlap bag toward the river. The head and front half, covered by the bag, hung limp, but two large, white paws and a big, bushy tail dangled out the open end. The tail was motionless. Ti'caw froze.

It isn't Ghost, she told herself. *It's just a stray.* She turned away, fighting back the waves of emotion crashing over her. When she turned around to look again there was nothing to see. The men had gone.

"There's nothing to say--nothing to tell anyone. I imagined it," Ti'caw told herself. This was her life now. Nothing would change that.

CHAPTER TWENTY-TWO

It was the end of the Moon of Falling Leaves when Lawala Clough blew ash from her white peaks and Tuck-na-wit shot the arrow into the bear's eye. Naha and Lala put Tarak to bed and fussed over his wounds like a pair of mama birds, making hot poultices of pounded root pulp and smearing the angry claw marks with warmed conifer pitch. Se'ahost was called in. He nodded and told the women they had done well then sat down and helped himself to Lala's food and Siniuse's tobacco.

When Tuck-na-wit told the story, he did not leave Tarak's part out. Though he was the hero of his tale, he let it be known that his slave, Tuck-na-wit's Friend, had taken part in saving the family's only surviving son. The villagers of Gualsquo understood this was a serious debt that could not easily be repaid, and everyone waited to see what the family would do.

During the weeks Tarak lay in bed healing, the sun traveled farther to the south, becoming too weak to burn through the heavy, grey clouds of the Pacific Northwest winter. Day after day it rained. The villagers hunched their backs against the wet, covered their heads with their blankets and stayed

CHAPTER 22

inside their long houses. Men smoked pipes and told the tales only told in winter, while women busied their hands with bead or quillwork. Children played and listened.

While he lay healing, Tarak dreamed he walked again in his village home beneath Wai-i-ka, safe among his family. But though he saw and heard them, they could not see or hear him. A fog separated them.

Tarak found this very hard, for there were many things he now wished to say to his parents.

I should have been a better son, Mother. I would be happy to carry water and wood for you. I should have been happy to do it then.

And I should have listened to you, Father, when you told me how important it was for a man to be patient.

Tarak worried too. His parents seemed changed. A sadness lingered in the corners of A'ni's smile and the hair at his father's temples was touched with gray. Only half of the men Ata' had grown up with had lived through the raid. The responsibility of providing meat for the village now lay with those who remained. It was proving to be a hard winter.

Though Tarak was invisible to his parents, there were times when he was sure that Iri'wa looked right at him--that she could see him.

"Where are you, Tarak? When are you coming home?" her eyes asked. *"Have you found your white shadow yet?"* Tarak had the feeling the

old woman was waiting for him to do something. But what? Questions hounded his mind.

Where was Ghost? Had it been him fighting the bear, or had it just been a spirit that Tarak's mind changed to look like his friend?

When Naha and Lala decided that Tarak was well enough, Tuck-na-wit's cousins and their friends came to visit, begging to hear the story of the bear attack. Day after day they came, asking for the same story and Tarak told it, but he never said anything about the white blur that had stopped the bear's second swipe at him, saving his life. The story was Tuck-na-wit's victory and Tarak left it at that.

When he was able to get up and move around the village again, Tarak discovered that the bear attack had changed his status in Gulasquo. The old men who smoked with Siniuse suddenly acknowledged his existence, nodding to him when they met. The younger children tagged along behind him, their eyes filled with admiration. Everyone knew him as Tuck-na-wit's Friend, and they greeted him like one of their own, inviting him into their lodges. Only Siniuse still treated Tarak like a slave.

But Tarak did not feel as if he belonged among the Gulasquo now, any more than he had the first day he came. He had not done anything brave or courageous or special to earn his new importance; Ghost had done it. Embarrassed, he

CHAPTER 22

did not seek the praise of others, preferring to sit quietly alone.

"The bear attack has changed you," Lala announced a few days after he was up and about again. "You are different."

Tarak shook his head. He could not see how, except for the scars across his chest. "All that has changed is the way others see me., Lala. I have not changed."

"No." Lala shook her head, lowering her voice to a whisper. "You're tamanawas is different, now, Friend. It is stronger, deeper. You feel things and think about them. Spirit has touched you. The tillicum see it."

With the Winter Ceremonies coming up fast, Siniuse and Tuck-na-wit were often away on trading trips, returning with beautiful baskets, shells, hides and trade blankets. Many fine gifts would be given at Tuck-na-wit's Naming Ceremony.

One day while the men were away, Tarak slipped out of the lodge alone and walked up the hill to the site of the bear attack.

The sounds of the village faded behind him, falling away into the mist that hung heavy over the sodden, leaf-covered ground. The bright green of moss and ferns stood out boldly against the frost-bitten vines and brambles. Tarak climbed the hill, breathing carefully so as not to stretch the scabs on his chest. The bare branched woods turned to pine forest then the trees opened up and Tarak was once again looking up at the cliff and the ledge above it where the coyote had its cave.

"Ghost? Where are you old friend?" A tear trickled down Tarak's cheek. Slowly, he walked the ground in circles, searching for any sign that what he had seen had been real, but rain and the curious had long since destroyed any tracks except their own.

"Ghost?" he called, plaintively, his sadness echoing through the trees. "Ghost, I'm here. Where are you, boy? Ghost?"

Something rustled among the trees and he turned. "Ghost, is that you, boy?" There was no answer. "Is someone there?" The forest remained silent.

Numb to everything but his own loss, Tarak sat on a stump, letting his tears fall; shivering in the rain.

"Tarak, what are you doing out here all alone, in the rain?" Big Woman's plump fingers touched the boy's cold face. Rain dripped from Tarak's hair, making threads of water run down his shirt. "You've only just gotten out of bed, lemolo boy. Lala and Naha didn't save you from the bear's scratches so you could die from the cold and damp." Big Woman pulled Tarak into the circle of warmth made by her generous size.

"I had to look for him." Tarak's teeth chattered.

"Look for who? The bear? He's not here. His hide is curing in the smokehouse."

CHAPTER 22

"No. Not the bear, Big Woman, my dog, Ghost."

The slave woman sighed. "Ah. The imaginary white dog again."

"He's not imaginary. He's real and he was here."

"He was real, Tarak, when you were back home on Wai-i-ka. Now he's just something your heart misses and wishes to see."

"But I saw him," Tarak insisted firmly. "He fought the bear--he saved us."

Big Woman shook her head. "I've heard the story of the arrow and the bear's eye and the coyote's cave a dozen times, Tarak; everyone in the village has. It's even being told in other villages along the river. I've heard the story from your own lips, more than once and not once have I ever heard anything about a white dog, not from you, not from Tuck-na-wit, not fom anybody."

"But Tuck didn't see Ghost," Tarak explained. "The ash from the mountain hid him. You could hardly see anything the ash was so thick."

"And with all that ash you could barely see the bear and yet, you saw a white dog?"

Tarak nodded. "It was right after Tuck hit it with the arrow. The bear was mad and he was going to hit me again, but Ghost came out of nowhere and jumped on him and pulled the bear away." Big Woman shook her head. "We were in the coyote's cave and the bear had the arrow its eye, but it was still alive, so why didn't it come after us? Because Ghost was keeping it away from us. Ghost killed it, not Tuck-na-wit."

"Tuck-na-wit's arrow was in its eye, Tarak. It took time for it to thrash around, but it was the arrow in its eye that killed the bear."

It was no use arguing. There wasn't even enough proof for him to convince himself. Maybe Big Woman was right; maybe he had just wished it was true.

"We have to get you back." Big Woman pulled Tarak to his feet. "If Siniuse thinks you've run away, he will punish you--bear or no bear."

"Big Woman, how did you know where to find me?" Tarak asked as they walked back to the village.

"Ti'caw saw you and came to tell me."

"Oh." It had been a long time since he had thought about Ti'caw. Tarak looked back to where he had seen Ghost fighting the bear but the only ghosts he saw now were the ghosts of memories and he could not trust them.

*****

The day for departure to Ka Klasco was bright and clear. A sunny day in the winter along the gorge was a rare treat and the travelers' spirits were high. Last minute preparations were finished and bundles tied to be carried to the canoes. Instructions were given to those who would stay

CHAPTER 22

behind; the elderly, the sick, those who were too young to travel and those who would stay to care for them.

It took two canoes to hold the teepee poles, hides, kitchen supplies, gifts and the food for Siniuse's family. A third canoe would carry the family themselves, the slaves and the overflow of gifts.

"Chako, alta. Move, lazy girl!" Ti'caw's mistress waddled up the riverbank waving her stubby hands at the reed-thin slave girl struggling under her load of bundles.

Tarak hardly recognized Ti'caw. Her back was curved like a stake that had been pounded into the earth and broken off. Her long, black hair was a shaggy, mud-caked matt. Scars and bruises blotched her skin and her bare feet were blue from the cold. There were more holes than wool in the thin blanket that hung from her shoulders.

Ti'caw looked up and their eyes met. Embarrassed, she looked away.

They had never been friends but Ti'caw was one of his own people, a part of him; the only link Tarak still had left to his old life, and that meant more to him now than any growl between them. He took off the fine wool blanket Tuck-na-wit had given him for their journey, walked over and placed it around Ti'caw's shoulders. She flinched, cowering away from him at the unexpected touch.

"It's okay, Ti'caw. It's just me, Tarak," he said, softly.

Blank, fearful, eyes looked back into his.

Tarak had never known the right words with Ti'caw and he struggled to find them now.

"I am sorry to see how hard your life is, but I want you to know that you are not invisible. You are still a person. I see you, Ti'caw. "His voice cracked, remembering how hollow he had felt when he thought no one saw him or cared about what happened to him.

Ti'caw did not smile back.

"Remember how you slapped that Snake's hand in the meadow the day they came for us?" Tarak tried again. "I was never so proud to be Kama'twa as I was when you did that. You were very brave." He did not know why he said it, or where the words had come from. He only knew that he longed to see some spark of that girl again in Ti'caw's eyes.

Ti'caw's thin, blue hand trembled as she touched the soft blanket.

"She will not let me keep this."Her voice was a ragged whisper. "My mistress will take it for herself or give it to one of the children." She began to take it off her shoulders. Tarak stopped her.

"You could hide it somewhere and only get it out at night when no one will see."

Ti'caw shook her head. "She will find it and be angry. Then she will beat me." Her voice

CHAPTER 22

caught on a sob. "I am not allowed anything of my own. Not even the body you see is mine anymore."

A clenched fist closed in Tarak's chest. "No one can take your spirit, Ti'caw," he insisted. "It is too strong. Don't forget that, girl. Remember who you are."

"You say that to me?" Tears spilled from Ti'caw's eyes. "You think because you give me a blanket, I will forgive you for everything? For all this?" She waved her arm. "For Chiwa'chni? Well, I won't. I will never forgive you, Tarak." She pulled the blanket from her shoulders and held it out to him. "Here. I don't want it."

Tarak took the blanket, rolled it up and stuffed it into one of the bundles at Ti'caw's feet. "Do whatever you want with it--throw it in the mud or tear it to pieces if you want, but it is yours. I gave it to you and I hope you will use it, even if it is only for one night, because that night you will sleep warm. I cannot undo what has been done, Ti'caw. I can only try to show you how sorry I am and that I have changed. I am not the boy I was that day any more than you are the same girl. If I could go back, I would not leave you again."

Ti'caw's lips quivered then her jaw set and her eyes turned hard. "I heard about the bear. You're a fool, Tarak. Why would you risk your life to save the one who calls you his slave?"

Tarak did not know how to make Ti'caw understand.

"Tuck-na-wit is my friend."

Ti'caw shook her head. "No, he is your master. Don't be fooled by warm hides and flattery. No matter what they say, you are something they bought and own and if they keep you, or throw you away no one will care."

"It's not like that with us," Tarak argued.

"No? You think you are equals now because Tuck-na-wit and his naha give you a nice place to sleep and food to fill your belly? If you really believe that, tell him you want to go home and ask him to set you free."

Tarak hung his head.

"If they were truly grateful for what you did, they'd set you free. They owe you a life debt. Everyone in the village knows it." She picked up the bundle at her feet. "Tuck-na-wit might call you 'Friend,' but he will never let you go." She headed down the beach to load her mistress's canoe, but she had kept the blanket.

Tuck-na-wit joined Tarak.

"Where's your new blanket, Friend?"

Tarak watched Ti'caw's thin figure. She had buried her proud spirit deep inside her beaten body, but it was still there. He had seen it.

"I gave it away in a friendship ceremony," he answered.

"Lemolo, siwash." Tuck-na-wit shook his head as they walked up the bank and into the camp. "Never mind. We will find you another one." He put an arm around Tarak's shoulder.

CHAPTER 22

"I do not want to go with you upriver, Tuck." The words danced on the tip of Tarak's tongue. *"I do not want to go to your Winter Ceremony. I want to find Ghost and go home.*

CHAPTER TWENTY-THREE

It was The Moon of Heavy Snows. The Christians at the Fort were just finishing their Christmas celebrations as the tillikum prepared for their winter ceremonies. Goose, wild turkey, ham, venison and even some of the precious new beef, raised on Company lands, had graced the Chief Factor's holiday table, along with a guest list made up of the territory's most important citizens.

When weather was good, the tillikum visited and traded along the river, but outside of the upcoming winter gathering at Ka'klasco, the focus of most trade now shifted to Fort Vancouver.

Company trappers traveled the back country up and down the Pacific Coast, traveling inland as far as snow allowed, in search of animals with heavy winter coats that would bring the best prices. In the spring, they would return to the fort with bundles of pelts to be shipped to London, Boston, and the hubs of European fashion, but furs were no longer the Fort's only business. Fifteen hundred acres were tilled each year and planted in wheat, barley and corn. The Company had pasturelands on both sides of the lower Columbia River, the white men's name for the Great River,

CHAPTER 23

and there were acres of fruit, nuts and vegetable gardens.

McLoughlin's Fort Vancouver was known as the "London of the west." The vista from "Belle Vue", the knoll it sat atop, was lush, green lands with mountains and valleys stacked one behind the other, parading into the distance. But this was not the fort's original location. The entire fort operation had been moved to this second site when the first was found to be poorly placed.

A twenty foot high stockade wall surrounded the new fort, boasting towers with cannons at the Northwest and Southwest corners. During John McLoughlin's time as Chief Factor, the cannons were never fired.

Fort Vancouver's walls enclosed a comfortable, orderly world that had everything the transplanted Europeans and their families felt was needed for a "civilized" life; a bakery, a church, a school. There was a community kitchen where Company cooks fed those workers who did not have families or wives to cook for them. There were warehouses to store furs and trade supplies, manufacturing buildings and a storehouse for weapons. Clapboard buildings lined two central "greens" seasonally planted as gardens, their paths lined with strawberries. Children attended school and did their sums, while women practiced needlework, beadwork, or quilting. They did the family baking, cared for their husbands, and raised the young. Officers of the Company were partners in the profits and under McLoughlin's leadership, profits were good. But the independence the British- owned Hudson's Bay Company had invested in, was a matter of self interest in their own profits. They had no desire to see the Pacific Northwest settled, especially by American pioneers who would work to make the area part of the United States and they were less than pleased with their Chief Factor's charitable support of the American settlers.

Outside the fort's walls, there was yet another transplanted world. "Kanaka" village had been named for the many Polynesian's the Hudson's Bay Company employed, who did not live inside the fort's walls. An early model for diversity, the community was a multi-cultural soup made up of Polynesians, Russians, the British, the French and local Natives from up and down the river.

The sound of metal striking metal ricocheted between Kanaka village's low buildings. Horses whinnied; side stepped, and sloshed through the mud, while dogs barked at those passing by, especially a large, white dog being dragged along by a man pulling on a rope.

The sharp tang of the village's smells stung Ghost's nose as he jerked and twisted, winding the rope that held him around his captor's legs.

"Stop it, you lemolo kamooks." Rufus yanked Ghost back around.

CHAPTER 23

Ghost coughed, choked by the rope around his neck, but he kept on moving, trying to see what made every noise. There were too many people, all of them strangers.

"Hurry and get the blanket set up, MacPhearson," Rufus ordered his companion. "I want a good spot. Hey, Kanaka man," he called out to a Hawaiian butcher he knew. "Can I use one of those cages you have out back for the hogs? This white devil has already chewed through two good ropes."

"Maybe he don't like stinky traders." The butcher grinned showing his red betel nut stained teeth.

"I'll be happy to sell him to someone he likes better."

"Empty cage behind the shop." The man tossed his head toward the back.

Leaving Ghost with MacPhearson, Rufus, hurried around to the alley that ran behind the shops.

Rufus Jackson called himself a trader but those who called him a thief and a scoundrel were more right than wrong. In his own mind, he was no different from anyone else. He was just trying to get by. Most people, however, were not willing to steal, cheat, or kill just to get by. It took a particular kind of person for that and Rufus Jackson was that kind of person. He had no loyalty or liking for anyone but himself and anyone who thought they were his friend was wise to watch their back.

The start of the Winter Ceremonies at Ka'klasco was only a few days away now, and Rufus needed a grubstake. There was trading to be done among the Indians upriver, far from the watchful eye of the Company, and large profits for those with no scruples and no stake in maintaining good relations with the Natives. But business had not been good for Rufus lately. His trade bags were almost empty and none of it was worth much. He needed a windfall.

Sauntering down the alley, Rufus took in the state of shop windows, doors and the conditions of their locks, looking for weaknesses he could use to his advantage. All he needed was a little luck. As he was dragging the hog cage back to where he'd left MacPhearson and the dog, he got it.

Doc Gairdner, the Company's physician, came walking down the street toward him. Rufus' pulse quickened. Doc Gairdner had helped him before, though the good doctor didn't know it. The good doctor had been a major player in the burglary of several of his patients over the last six months.

"Hey, Doc," Rufus hailed the doctor. "It's good to see you." He grabbed the doctor's hand and pumped it with a show of enthusiasm.

"Ah, Mr. Jackson. I'm afraid you catch me at a bad moment, sir. I cannot tarry," Gairdner apologized.

CHAPTER 23

"On your way to help the sick? You're a saint. Where is it they're sending you this time?"

"I'm just returning from a small farm on the Deschutes. Some settlers, the Stantons, have been taken ill. Do you know them?"

"Cabin on the east bank, a couple of miles from the Columbia?" Rufus picked a random cabin.

Gairdner blinked. "No. Their place is upriver on the West side."

Rufus nodded. "Oh yeah, I remember now. Them rivers, the way they twist and turn around sometimes I can't tell where I'm at until I see a familiar face smiling at me and inviting me in for a sit. I been by there," he lied smoothly. "Nice folks. So, they gonna be okay, Doc?"

"God willing. I can't say for certain yet." Gairdner sighed. "It looks like the fever."

Rufus clicked his tongue sympathetically, but his eyes sparked with greed. "Well, that's a darn shame. I'll be praying' for them, I will."

"Thank you. Sometimes that's all a good Christian can do."

"I better not keep you, Doc. You look plum done in." The trader tipped his hat and resumed pulling the cage along the street. As soon as he got it to the trading grounds, he shoved the white dog inside and tied the door shut.

"That'll show you. And there you'll stay 'till someone gives me something shiny to take you out." He kicked the cage so Ghost jumped. Rufus turned to the small collection of mismatched items set out on the shabby blanket, mentally counting what he could expect to make. He needed passage upriver and a nest egg for at least one. MacPhearson, like others before him, was disposable. Dumb as a stump, the man's only skill was his strong back and in the Oregon territory backs came cheap.

Rufus picked his teeth with a twig. Even on a good day, what he had would not be enough. But that didn't really matter anymore, because just upriver there was a farmhouse full of sick people who were probably going to die in a day or so. All he had to do was get there and take advantage of the situation.

A few people began to slow down and take a look at what was on the blanket, a couple of them bargaining for smaller, useful items. Eager to move on to better pickings, Rufus made them better deals than usual. Still, it was in his nature to try to get a dime out of a nickel.

He noticed a young half blood watching the caged dog from across the street. After a bit the fellow strolled over to the cage and stuck his hand inside, letting the dog sniff it.

"Be careful," Rufus warned. "He's a guard dog, that one." As if to make a fool of him, the white dog stretched out his tongue and licked the Indian's hand.

"Hey there, Skookum," Jimmy Buckeye whispered. "How'd you get yourself here?" He

CHAPTER 23

looked over Ghost's wounds, old and new. "Been fighting, eh? Well, I hope it was worth it 'cause it looks like you paid a good price for the honor."

Rufus sidled over to the cage, chewing on a wad of tobacco.

"He's some dog, eh?"

Jimmy nodded.

"A dog like that don't come around every day. He's almost as big as some donkeys down south but a lot easier to get along with." Rufus spit the tobacco wad into the mud. "Some of them donkeys got tempers you just can't deal with no how. This one'll do what you say though, 'long as you know how to keep the upper hand." He kicked the cage again. Ghost snarled. "Seems to have taken to you though."

Rufus squinted his eyes up, judging his customer. "You interested in making me an offer?"

"Where'd you find him?" Jimmy asked, his jaw clenched.

"What do you mean 'find' him? I raised this dog from a pup. Had him since he was weaned from his mother's teat." Truth had never held much interest for Rufus. If he had any talent at all, it was making up a lie on the spot and believing it just as quick.

Jimmy raised his eyebrows. "Really? You don't say."

"So you want to buy him? He's a big dog--a hard worker. I'd keep him myself, only I can't bear to look at him, since his old mam died. Almost the picture of her, he is and it just 'bout breaks my heart."

"I can see that." Jimmy said, his sarcasm lost on the trader. "He's wounded."

Rufus shrugged. "He fights. That's why I put him in a cage. Maybe you want him for fighting, eh? He's as strong as the devil. In a few weeks, he'll be ready to take on a bear. You could win a lot of bets fighting this dog."

Jimmy Buckeye's face clouded over like a storm. "You dirty scum."

"What did you call me?" Rufus bristled.

"I know this dog," Jimmy said. "'Kind of hard to believe, you having raised him from a pup and all, but my partner, Loo-ee Barbo and I rescued Skookum here, when we were trapping in the mountains down south, last summer. Someone had shot him with an arrow. See, here's the scar."

Rufus licked his lips. "You work for the Company?"

"Been with 'em for years."

Rufus' eyes darted back and forth. The last thing he needed right now was problems with the Company.

"That dog's been nothing but trouble since we picked him up," Macphearson grumbled.

"Shut up, Mac."

Jimmy looked Rufus in the eye. "So, I'm gonna ask you again, and maybe this time your memory will be better. Where did you find this dog?"

CHAPTER 23

"He was a stray beggin' for food outside some village upriver. He was starvin'. Anybody could see he didn't belong to nobody."

"Well, he sure doesn't belong to you."

"Look, I don't want any trouble," Rufus whined. "But I've been feedin' and takin' care of this big guy for weeks now," Rufus lied. "He was in a really bad way when I took him in all crazy with hunger. I saved his life and he pretty much just 'caused me a mess of trouble--ate right through two good ropes. You can have the dog back if you want, but I deserve something for my expenses. It's only fair."

"Sort of like a reward for finding him or something?"

"Yeah, that's it; a reward. You give me a reward and you take the dog and everyone's happy."

"How much do you think would be fair for this reward?" Jimmy asked.

Rufus could smell money now. The man wanted the dog. He named a large sum.

Jimmy's face turned red. "You're lemolo. I could feed a whole village for a month for that."

Rufus shrugged. "I have the dog in a cage. I can just keep him there and see who else comes to claim him. Maybe someone else thinks he's their dog. How do I know what you say is true?"

"Hey, Angus!" Jimmy called the big Scot over. "You remember this dog?"

E.F.WINTERS

"Sure; Skookum, right? He was with you at Silaylo. Did you sell him?"

Jimmy smiled at Rufus, triumphantly. "No, I did not sell him." Angus McDonald was well known at the Fort. His word would count for a lot against a con man like Rufus Jackson. Rufus licked his lips nervously.

"I outa' get somethin'" he whined.

"What are you doin' Jimmy?" Angus asked. "You buyin' your own dog? Hey Skookum!" he called out. Ghost barked in reply. "See there? It's the man's dog, no question."

"I ain't arguin' that," Rufus protested. "He's just givin' me a reward for its safe return is all."

Jimmy nodded, taking paper money with the Hudson's Bay insignia on it out of his purse.

Angus grinned wide. "Well then, I guess it's all settled. I'll just get the old kamooks out of that cage. I don't think he likes it much in there." Angus loosened the knotted rope. Before he had even opened the cage door, Ghost pushed past him, and bolted away through the crowd.

"Skookum! Skookum, come back!" Jimmy called, running after him.

Angus shook his head. "That dog doesna' think he belongs to anyone," he muttered.

"Pack up," Rufus ordered his companion. "We're headed upriver. We're gonna visit some folks I know who is sick on the Deschutes."

CHAPTER TWENTY-FOUR

By the time Tuck-na-wit's family arrived at Ka-klasco, most of the visitor's had already made camp. The smoke from hundreds of fires puffed out from top knots made of the bunched ends of long teepee poles rose up into the winter blue sky. The village's weather-bleached longhouses looked tired and faded beside the brightly painted teepees.

As families arrived, men folk went in search of friends to share news and a smoke, while the women and slaves hauled the supplies up from the canoes and set up the teepees. Leaving the female slaves to the task, Tuck-na-wit took Tarak to explore the camp.

Shouts and clouds of dust rose from the eastern edge of the camp, loud whoops underscoring the barking of dozens of dogs.

"Chako! Chako, Friend!" Tuck began to run. "They're coming!"

As the boys entered the center of the village, men in fringed buckskin with eagle feather bonnets galloped down the main path, waving weapons and shouting.

"Ya-la-la-la-la-la!"

Tarak grabbed Tuck-na-wit to spin him out of the way, his heart pounding sure that the village was under attack but no one was running away. Instead, they were gathering to watch.

"It is the Kikiya arriving." Tuck-na-wit's eyes shone, his cheeks flushed with excitement. "Aren't they wonderful?" The riders waved and called out to friends, the village dogs circling their horse's legs, yipping and snapping. "They enter like this every year. Father says they just like to show off, but I think it's the best part of the gathering. We're so late, I thought we'd missed them but we were just in time."

Tarak tried to breathe more deeply and slow his racing heart.

"They're very...loud," he mumbled, trying to cover his embarrassment.

One of the Kikiya, a big bear of a man, rode a beautiful spotted horse. The crowd cheered when he jumped over its back from one side to the other. He was clearly a favorite.

"Kamiakin." Tuck-na-wit sighed with admiration. "He is a great man among the tillikum, known from the Great River all the way to the Great Plains."

"Klosh sun." Tuck-na-wit's uncle joined the boys.

"Klosh sun, Tot," Tuck greeted him in return.

"Are you ready to go to the trading grounds to finish buying for your give-away?"

"Chako." Tuck-na-wit turned to Tarak, shaking the strings of shells wound around his arm.

CHAPTER 24

"Naha has given me dentalia shells to trade for the last of my potlatch." They headed toward the market area.

Blankets displayed the usual metal tools, hides, sugar salmon, and oolichan, an oily fish that burned like a candle, as well as more unusual items like chil chil; the small beads white men called buttons.

Tuck-na-wit picked up a delicately painted tea cup.

"That's china. Kloshe nanitch. It breaks like a bird's egg." The trader warned.

Tuck-na-wit made a face. "It is made so poorly?"

The trader laughed. "No. It is supposed to be like that."

"Why would a person want such a thing?"

"Klootchman ticky. Women like the pretty flowers." The man winked. "Little siwash can huy huy for his sweetheart, eh?"

Tuck-na-wit frowned. "I am not little. I am going to be named a man at the ceremonies. I am looking for a gift for my naha."

"Oh, your naha. Well, mama's ticky china." The trader turned the cup so Tuck-na-wit could see the dainty flowers and gold edges. The lip was as thin as a leaf.

"I don't think so." Tuck-na-wit shook his head, his attention caught by another trader's display. A bright red length of material hung from a tree branch, its fringe rippling in the faint breeze.

"What about that?" Tuck walked to the tree. The fringe edging the material trickled over his fingers like water. "I have never seen a blanket like this before."

Tot came up behind him. "They call these paseessee, shawls. White women wear them. Hyas Tee's wife wears one all the time."

"She is not a white woman," Tuck argued.

"No, she is Metis, but she dresses like a white woman."

The faded blanket marking out the trader's space was covered with used household goods.

"Ticky mahcook? Do you want to trade?" The rank odor of the trader's nervous sweat oozed from his pasty skin. Greasy brown hair hung around his face and his body moved as if it had no bones. Tarak did not like being near him.

"Maybe we should look some more. There are many traders, Tuck." Tarak touched his freind's shoulder.

Tuck-na-wit pulled away.

"No. I am not ready." He was enchanted by the red paseessee. "Kunsih? How much?" he asked.

"Oh, red paseesscc big dolla," the trader's lips popped the words out through the gap in his rotting teeth, rolling a stinky wad of chewing tobacco around his mouth.

"Kunsih?" Tuck-na-wit repeated, his nose wrinkling in disgust at the trader's bad smell.

The man's eyes shifted greedily to the string of shells winding around Tuck-na-wit's arm.

CHAPTER 24

"It is very rare. Made of special material called silk." The trader's dirty hand stroked the soft fabric. "It comes from a far off land over the Great Water. You can't get silk like this just anywhere."

Tuck-na-wit put his hand out and let the soft material slide across the back of his hand. "Kunsih?"

The trader licked his lips. "Two dentalia strings."

Tot spit on the ground. "Hyas mahcook. He's trying to cheat you, nephew. Chako. Let's go."

Tuck-na-wit did not move. "No. I want the silk pasessee for Naha."

"It would take almost all you have, and you have other gifts to buy."

Tuck-na-wit folded his arms across his chest. "But I want it."

"And he knows that," Tot hissed. "Walk away and you will get a better price."

Tuck-na-wit frowned.

"Tenas paseessee." Tarak frowned, shaking his head. "It's too small, Tuck. This silk won't keep Naha warm. There are better things over there." Tarak winked as he pointed to another blanket farther down the line.

Tuck-na-wit caught on to the game. "You are right, Friend. This one is too much dolla for something so useless. Maybe Naha would ticky china."

Tarak nodded. "China is kloshe. Klootchman like it."

Another buyer, a white man, began looking at the trader's blanket. Sensing he had lost Tuck-na-wit's business, the trader shifted his attention to this new prospect.

"See anything you like, sir? I'll give you a good price," he oozed.

The man picked up a carved stone that hung from a ribbon and his face paled. "Where did you get this?"

The trader's eyes grew round, shifted and he turned back to Tuck-na-wit.

"Not so fast, son," he called Tuck back. "It's going to kill me but I've got a soft spot for mothers. Since the paseessee is potlatch for your naha, I'll make you a special deal; a string and a half and it's yours."

"Where did you get these things?" The other man raised his voice, looking at other items on the blanket.

"I will look at some other things first," Tuck-na-wit said firmly.

"I asked you where you got these things." The man picked up a hat, holding it as if it might bite him. "Where?" The trader continued ignoring him. The man grabbed the trader's shoulder and spun him around, shaking the hat in his face. "I asked you where you got these things."

The trader's eyes shifted between the angry man and Tuck.

CHAPTER 24

"Rufus? What's going on?" The trader's companion appeared.

"Shut up and start picking this stuff up," Jackson hissed. He turned to Tuck-na-wit. "Half a string. Tenas siwash--only five shells and mamook mahish. It's yours."

"Kloshe. We have a deal." Tuck pulled off the shells and gave them to the trader.

Rufus thrust the shawl at the boy and began frantically tossing goods into a bag.

The other buyer grabbed Rufus by the collar. "I demand you answer me, sir!"

"I-I don't know," the trader stammered, his eyes bulging. "People trade what they don't want for what they do. I don't remember where I get every little trinket."

"I know these things." The man let go of the trader's shirt, lifting a leather-bound book. "I knew the Stantons, to whom they belonged. You are a thief, sir! You've taken these goods from the cabins of the sick and unfortunate. You've stolen them from the dead!"

Rufus threw the last of the items into the bag and hurried away, the angry man running after him, still shouting.

Tuck-na-wit and Tarak walked away. This growl between white men had nothing to do with them.

CHAPTER TWENTY-FIVE

Tuck-na-wit's wide smile stretched his moon-face even rounder.

"When I dance, I will become Bear." He swayed and stomped, mimicking a bear's lumbering gait. The back of the bear hide draped over him and curved as he dropped onto his hands and knees. Beneath the hide, Tuck-na-wit wore a leather loincloth, his bare chest and arms painted with sacred symbols.

"Did you ever imagine such a night?" He took a deep breath, thrusting his chest out. "Tonight, I become a man. Hyea"! He shouted jubilantly. "Tonight, I will get my grown up name and my tamanawas will be revealed to everyone. Tonight, my father will show everyone how proud he is of his second son." Tuck-na-wit held up a small leather pouch that hung around his neck. "See this, Friend? This is big magic. Naha made it for me to keep the sacred things the tawati will give me at the ceremony." Tuck-na-wit spun, slicing the air with the bear hide. He struck a warrior's pose, his face set in a fierce copy of his father's.

Lala snorted as she stepped in past the tent flap.

CHAPTER 25

"A man? Ha! You still sleep in your naha's tent." She filled her arms with another load of gifts for the ceremony.

Tuck-na-wit scowled. "Only because I choose to. I could sleep anywhere I wanted after tonight." He removed the bear hide, trading it for the new elk-hide cape his mother had made for him. The mink tails she had sewn along its edge dragged across the floor. "I don't even have to go to sleep at all anymore if I don't want to. I can stay up and dance all night and no one can say anything about it."

Lala let go a pungent fart. The boys looked at each other and fell back laughing onto their bed.

"A-de-dah! Mamook klatawa, she makes a mighty wind!" They joked.

The slave woman pretended nothing had happened. "Your naha is on her way to fetch you, big man."

"Is the red pasessee with the other gifts?" Tuck-na-wit asked.

"Yes, it is there," Lala assured him for the twentieth time.

"And the offerings for the tawati and the speaker?"

"Everything is ready. It may be your first naming ceremony but it is not mine. Did you give Friend the new belt pouch I made?"

Tuck looked embarrassed as he trotted over to a basket and took out a small leather bag.

"This is for you." He handed it to Tarak.

Lala smiled and winked. Tuck-na-wit might be the one handing it to him but he knew who the gift was really from. He ran his hand over the soft leather, fingering the precise beadwork. It was not as fancy as something the only son of a wealthy family might have but few slaves would have something as nice.

"It is a very good bag. Thank you, Tuck." Tarak added a silent smile for Lala. She added one last item to the top of the pile in her arms and waddled out.

Tuck-na-wit turned to Tarak.

"I wish you could dance beside me. I have asked Sowapso to cut three lines across my chest, here." He motioned a sideways swipe from one side of his chest to the other. "To match the bear's claw marks on your chest; to honor you as my brother, because you helped me." He lifted his chin. "I will not cry out when the knife cuts my skin. I will be brave so everyone will know that I am truly a man of tamanawas."

"Your family will be very proud." Tuck-na-wit had called him his brother, but Tuck-na-wit would become a man tonight and Tarak would remain a slave. The encouraging smile he gave his friend did not come easy. Envy and disappointment circled each other at the edges of Tarak's heart.

Ti'caw had said that people in the village were waiting to see how the family would repay the debt they owed Tarak for saving their only remaining son. Tarak had hoped this would be the

CHAPTER 25

night he was given that gift and it would be his freedom, but it felt as if the moment had come and gone.

"Tuck-na-wit, chako! It is time," Naha called from outside the teepee.

Tuck-na-wit raced to the door. "Has Sowapso agreed to everything, Naha?"

His mother nodded, smiling the same broad smile as her son.

"Yes, and the tawati, Smohalla, will be the crier. It is a great honor to have two such men do your naming. Come now, you dance first. We must not keep the tillikum waiting."

Tuck-na-wit took a deep breath. "I am ready."

Tarak stepped into line behind his master as usual but as he approached the door, Siniuse appeared, blocking the doorway.

"Slaves are not allowed."

"But he is my friend," Tuck-na-wit protested.

"Not tillikum." The hawk nosed man glowered down at Tarak.

"But I asked him to come, Father. I want him there. He is my brother now."

"He is not your brother," Siniuse barked. "He is a slave. A slave is not a person. It would be an insult to Sowapso and Smohalla. I am finished speaking about this." In a few long strides, Siniuse caught up with his wife, leaving Tuck-na-wit and Tarak alone in the teepee.

Tuck chewed at his bottom lip. "I will tell you all about it when I come back." He hesitated. "You will wait here for me, Friend, won't you?"

"Of course." Tarak nodded.

"Good. Then I will see you soon." He flashed Tarak a smile then hurried to join his parents.

Tarak stood in the doorway. On the far side of the camp, a slow rhythmic drumbeat began to vibrate the chill twilight. The boughs of the pine trees bounced, the needles quivering with the beat.

A light snow began to fall. Tillikum from all over the camp were making their way to the ceremonial lodge, leaving only the slaves outside, doing their chores. Tarak watched them carrying wood, hauling water and carrying bundles to their master's teepees and lodges. Without Tuck-na-wit beside him, Tarak had nothing to do; nowhere to go. He had no chores, and no purpose among the tillikum. His only chore was to be his master's shadow. Their lives had become one life: Tuck-na-wit's, and without him, Tarak had no place in this world.

His friend called them brothers but you could not be brothers with a non-person. When Tuck-na-wit came back as a man, with a man's rights, would he stand up to his father and force Siniuse to recognize Tarak as a person, or were Tuck's words just noisy air, like Lala's farts?

The camp emptied, anyone of importance had gone to the ceremony. Slaves hurried inside to

CHAPTER 25

sit by fires, grabbing a few precious moments for themselves.

Tarak looked around. He could walk away right now and no one would even notice. There were piles of stores in the teepee. He could gather whatever he could carry and head South tonight. How far would he get before they came after him? How long would it be before they even realized he had gone? Tarak looked back at the ceremonial lodge.

"You will wait here for me, won't you Friend?"

Tarak had promised he would. Ti'caw would call him a fool but how could he leave now? The sound of the big drum reminded Tarak of the men's sweat house back home. His stomach knotted. Was Ti'caw right? Had his friendship with Tuck become a betrayal of his family? But Tuck was family, too now, wasn't he? Tot, Lala, Naha, and Big Woman were all a part of his life. Where did his loyalties lie? He did not know. Even asking the question added to Taraks confusion.

"Ghost. Where is Ghost?" Something deep inside him spoke.

"A few more days...I will stay a few more days. After we return to Gulasquo, once the weather changes, I will go."

Tarak followed the beat of the drum.

The cedar plank ceremonial lodge was the largest building in Ka'klasco; round, with a hole in the center for the smoke to escape. Tarak walked around the outside until he found a good sized crack between the planks. Putting his eye to it he looked inside. The tillikum were packed in like bunchgrass.

A long cedar pole, suspended vertically from a beam, swung slowly back and forth. When it struck a big pole in the lodge's framework, it made the deep booming that sounded like a hundred drums, making the forest dance.

An old man in a ceremonial robe sat on an elkhide covered platform, whispering under his breath.

Sowapso. Tarak thought, hardly daring to breathe. He was so close he could see the deep wrinkles in the holy man's face. The legendary Kikiya taught the "Dreaming Way", reminding the tillikum their traditional ways honored their ancestor's. The elder's breathy incantations became louder and Tarak could hear his words.

"The human beings gathered here call the mountains, the water and the fields, the animals and the creatures of the air, the ocean, the rivers, earth and the snow, the rain, sun, moon and stars, the old and the young, to witness that this person, who was a boy, has gone to the mountain and spoken with the Spirits," the holy man's words addressed all the nations of the world, but his voice did not carry to the back of the lodge. He stopped while another, younger man, repeated his words, in a loud, booming voice, so that all could hear them.

Smohalla.

CHAPTER 25

Tarak recognized the squat, hump-backed tawati from the fishing grounds at Silaylo Falls.

Sowapso went on, his voice a soft prayer then once again he waited while Smohalla repeated his words.

"The spirits have honored this person by giving him a dream that shows him a good way to live and they have given him a new name to help him remember this path." Smohalla sang out. "From this day forward this person will be known as Chet'woot; Black Bear; a man of the Gulasquo." Smohalla took his knife and sliced four shallow cuts across Tuck's chest, mirroring the scabs Tarak bore from the bear's claws.

Tuck–na-wit leapt around the stage roaring like a bear and pounding his feet against the boards of the stage. The leather string with one of the bear's claws attached to it, bounced against his chest.

"It is a great honor to hear the words of Sowapso," a voice spoke from behind Tarak. "Even if it is only through the cracks of a wall."

Tarak spun around, startled. The large man with the strong cheekbones, wide nose and generous mouth could not be mistaken for anyone but who he was. Kamiakin stood before him.

Tarak swallowed hard, wondering what the punishment for spying on a sacred ceremony would be.

"And who are you, young man, that you are left peeking in through a hole, instead of standing inside with the tillikum?" Humor softened the Kikiya warrior's features.

Tarak wetted his lips. "I am Tarak, from the high valleys of the Klamath River, Uncle. My people are the Kama-twa." He lowered his gaze, unable to look the great man in the eyes when he admitted his shame. "But here they call me Tuck-na-wit's Friend; from Gulasquo."

"Ah." Kamiakin nodded knowingly. "Then that one dancing inside is your brother. I have heard of you. But that does not explain why you are out here, when he is in there."

Tarak hesitated, biting his lip. "I am a slave; a non person. I am not allowed."

Kamiakin's eyebrows pulled together. "Who said so? All the tillikum are invited to the winter ceremonies."

"Siniuse said that my coming would be an insult to Sowapso and Smohalla."

"Siniuse says a lot of things." The Kikiya sat on a stump and pulled out his pipe. "But just saying something does not make it true. Not everyone agrees with him. I, for instance, think that we are ourselves, not what others say about us." He shrugged. "But, of course, a man can only speak his own heart." The Kikiya leader tamped a mixture of tobacco and willow bark into the bowl of his pipe. "Tell me, Tarak, what makes a boy into a man among the Kama-twa?" He struck a spark from a flint-rock and lit his pipe.

CHAPTER 25

"He kills a deer and then there is a ceremony—"

"Ceremonies do not make men." Kamiakin waved his hand dismissing the explanation as well as the ceremony going on inside the lodge.

Tarak dug his toes through the top layer of crusted snow into the soft powder beneath it. "That is what my grandfather said as well."

"We are not so different, my people and yours." Kamiakin formed his mouth into an "o" making smoke rings in the air. Tarak and Kamiakin watched as the circles drifted and disappeared.

"I travel among many people and among all that I have visited, if a person fights a bear and lives, he is a man." Kamiakin glanced at the neck of Tarak's tunic where the top edges of the scars from the bear's claws could be seen.

"Not a slave," Tarak pointed out.

Inside the ceremonial lodge, a man with a raspy voice began to sing.

"Do you hear that man singing?" Kamiakin asked, drawing on his long pipe. "He is called Tumsowit. He is tawati of Ka'Klasco. You understand this wa-wa, 'tawati'? It means an important person. Kumptus?"

Tarak nodded.

"But Tumsowit was not always called by this name. When he first came to the Great River he was a slave, like you. But no more. Tumsowit's tamanawas made him powerful among those who once thought themselves his masters. Now, all that is forgotten--unimportant. He is treated with respect and asked for advice in great matters. A strong heart is what makes a man, Tarak. Just as unselfish friendship creates a bond of brotherhood between two men. I have found that human beings everywhere recognize courage. Why do you think that is?"

"Because it is important?"

"Because it is rare. When you see someone with a great heart, it does not matter where they were born, or who they are, it does not even matter if they are a man or a woman. People know they are true human beings." Kamiakin set his pipe on the stump beside him, took his knife from its sheath and cut the sinew tying one of the eagle feathers in his hair.

"Tarak of the Kama-twa and the village of Gulasquo, I give you this gift in recognition not of what you have done, but for who you have become." Kamiakin took Tarak's hand and placed the feather on its open palm.

Tarak did not know what to say. There were no words in the Jargon that could speak what filled his heart.

"Mahish; thank you," he said, simply and honestly. When he looked up, Kamiakin was already disappearing into the ceremonial lodge. Tarak slipped the feather beneath his buckskin shirt, next to his skin. Its stiff quill scratched the scabbed wounds on his chest, but he did not mind.

CHAPTER 25

He felt as light as the feather that was settled over his heart.

He was not a slave. He was a man. Kamiakin had said it.

CHAPTER TWENTY-SIX

A fierce storm pushed up the river gorge, covering Ka'klasco in a foot and a half of deep, cold, snow. It piled up on the roofs of the longhouses and mounded outside the teepees in soft swells. Inside, festival visitors and their hosts huddled close to the fires, sharing news, gossip, and stories.

"Kamiakin brings word from our brothers in the East. The whites there have taken almost all of their lands," the elders chewed over the news passed on to them from the Nez Perce.

"Disease has killed even more of them there than here and those that remain are being pushed West, so whites can take their land." The elders shook their heads. But these were not the stories the young people wanted to hear.

"Tell the story of Raven and--"

"No, tell the story of Coyote," they clambered, and the elders set aside their worries and told the old stories that everyone knew and loved.

The winter days were short and many who had come to the festival slept all through the day to spend the long nights dancing and celebrating.

By late afternoon, the early twilight had drained the color from the sky. Tarak and Tuck-na-

CHAPTER 26

wit, who was now called Chet'woot, left the warmth of the longhouse where they had spent the afternoon and hurried through the bitter cold, headed for their own fire. As they approached the teepee, a line of women with blankets drawn around their shoulders came out, talking quietly to each other. White streaks dusted the dark hair of the youngest of them, while the oldest's shone like fresh snowdrifts in the evening light.

"Good evening, Aunties." The boys stood aside respectfully, until the women had passed. Inside, one old grandmother still stood by Naha's bed. In spite of the warm fire, a hollow silence chilled the air.

"This is not a sickness of our tillikum," the old woman explained to Lala. "It is a white men's disease. The medicines our grandmothers handed down to us have no power over it. I am sorry, Lala, there is nothing any of us can do. Maybe Konaway Se'ahost--?"

Lala spat on the ground. "Se'ahost is a fool."

The old woman shrugged. "Perhaps if Siniuse sent to the fort for the white doctin?" Lala's eyes pleaded for help the old woman could not give.

"You know he will not."

"I am sorry." The old woman shook her head and hobbled out into the night.

Tuck-na-wit clutched his new bear claw necklace. "Lala, what was the healer woman doing here? What did she mean, her medicines have no power? What is wrong with Naha?"

Lala rubbed her face with a weather worn hand. "Your naha is sick, Chet'woot."

Tuck-na-wit's face went ashen. "Is it…is it the fever like…?" His voice trailed off for he could not say his dead brother's name.

"I don't know what to do." Lala choked back tears. "Some say to bathe her in the river so the cold water will put out the fire inside her. Others say that when the people on the Willamette did that, it made people even sicker. There is no one here who knows what to do." She wrung her hands. "But the master's pride will never let us send for the white doctin." She looked up at Tuck-na-wit, her eyes growing wide with dismay. "I am sorry, Tuck--I mean Chet'woot. I should not have said that. Pay no attention to this foolish, old slave woman. I am just tired. Naha will be fine. I will take care of her and she will get well. There is stew in the pot over the fire." She poured a cup of pine tea and returned to her mistress' side.

Tuck-na-wit ate the stew that Tarak dished for him in silence then pulled the hide covering of his bed up over his head. The heavy hides almost muffled the soft sound of his crying.

Tarak lay awake for a long time. When he finally drifted into a troubled sleep he dreamed.

The world was dark with no light then out of the suffocating blackness fierce, yellow eyes, appeared, glowing malevolently with a deep,

CHAPTER 26

greedy, need. They rushed Tarak, rolling, tumbling and piling around him. Somewhere beyond them women wailed for their dead.

Kamiakin's feather floated toward Tarak. He reached out and grasped its thin, sharp quill, drawing it to him.

"When you see someone with a great heart, it does not matter where they were born, or who they are," Kamiakin's words whispered in his head. "It does not even matter if they are a man or a woman. People know them because they are true human beings."

The sharp prick of the eagle feather pressing against Tarak's chest woke him from his dream. He pulled the feather from its hiding place under his shirt and smoothed its delicate edge with his fingers. He had not shown it to anyone, not even Tuck.

"Breakfast is in the pot," Lala grunted.

Tarak slipped the feather back under his shirt and patted it flat before going to the cook-fire. Looking over at Naha, he thought how small and shrunken she looked under the large pile of blankets Lala had placed over her, as if the blankets could keep her safe from the illness that stalked her. The half moons beneath the sad woman's eyes were hollow and dark.

"Tell Siniuse I want to go home," the sick woman whispered to Lala, in a voice as fragile as the fall leaves decaying beneath the snow. "I want to sleep in my own lodge."

"I will tell him, mistress," Lala promised, the edges of her mouth quivering between encouragement and despair.

Within hours, the family was packed and headed back downriver.

Gulasquo village looked lonely among the leafless cottonwoods. Thin reeds of smoke rose from the lodges of those who had stayed behind.

"Chet'woot, keep your slave quiet," Siniuse commanded. "Naha must not be disturbed."

Tuck-na-wit looked at his mother lying in the bottom of the canoe, cocooned in blankets. "Yes, Papa."

Silence held Siniuse's lodge so close Tarak thought it would squeeze the breath from him. No visitors came to gossip or smoke. Lala moved like a shadow, silent and fearful. Siniuse sat like stone, slumped within himself. Tuck-na-wit and Tarak slipped in and out like skookums on the wind.

On the second morning after they had returned, Tarak did not wake to the smell of breakfast. The choking scent of ash was thick in the air. At the far end of the sleeping platform, Lala knelt beside her mistress. Tarak crawled out from under the hide covers and came quietly over to her.

"Auntie," he whispered, trying not to disturb the others. "You have been up all night again. You must rest. Let me stay with Naha while you sleep for a while."

Lala turned to Tarak, her eyes fogged with pain, tear tracks streaking the soot she had smeared

CHAPTER 26

over her cheeks and forehead. Her arms were covered with the dark gray powder. It sprinkled her dress and dusted the wooden platform around her knees. A pile of it lay cupped in her lap.

"There is no need anymore. She is gone." Lala's voice was as thin and taut as stretched sinew. "I have lived in this woman's lodge for twenty seven winters. She has been my friend and her life has been my life. What will I do now, Tarak? Where will I go? I am too old to learn the ways of a new mistress. Aaiiee. This life is too sad." She took the knife from her belt and sawed through one black braid then the other, dropping them onto the ash covered planks. "Stay with Chet'woot. He will need you." Lala's voice broke.

"I will," Tarak promised.

Lala scooped handfuls of ash from her lap and began rubbing it into her shorn hair, coating the black strands in a dull gray.

"Aieeeee. Aieeee." She rocked back and forth.

Tuck-na-wit and Siniuse woke to the sound of the slave woman, wailing this new sorrow.

For two days, Tarak sat beside Tuck-na-wit while his friend watched shadow and firelight dance across his mother's dead face, as if he could memorize every line and hold it in his heart for the rest of his days. On the third day, Tuck suddenly jumped to his feet and ran from the lodge. Tarak followed.

"I am sorry. I just had to get out of there." Tuck-n-wit's eyes and nose were red and streaming. "I couldn't take it anymore. I feel like my spirit is screaming and tearing at my insides. I just needed to move and breathe and remember what it is to be alive." His whole body was trembling. "I feel like it is me who has died. Like they are burying me. Do you understand, Friend? You must think I am weak." He turned away, tears rolling down his cheeks. "I just couldn't take it anymore."

"Let's go for a walk and get away for a bit?" Tarak suggested.

Snow still blanketed the nearly empty village but more of the tillikum returned from upriver everyday and packed snow paths led to most of the common areas. Tuck-na-wit and Tarak avoided these, wandering instead into the woods where they would not meet anyone or have to face the questions in their eyes or see their fear.

At first, they walked in a silence heavy with grief, but after awhile, they began to talk about small, unimportant things--things that were not terrible or sad. The short winter afternoon slipped away too quickly and sundown found the two friends lingering on a fallen log near the village's East end. Tuck shivered, his knees pulled up to his chest. His leather pant legs were wet and beginning to freeze as the temperature dropped.

CHAPTER 26

"Maybe we should go back," Tarak suggested. "It's getting dark. It's not good for you—"

"Who do you think you are telling me what to do?" Tuck-na-wit snapped, unexpectedly. "You are not my naha. You are not my older brother." He wiped a hand under his nose. "You are just a slave boy my papa bought so I would stop being sad, but it didn't work. My brother is dead and now my mother is dead too!" Frozen tears puckered the skin on Tuck-na-wit's round cheeks. "Why does everyone I care about die? My tamanawas is cursed."

Tarak stood and slowly began walking back to the lodge. Before he got there, Tuck's footsteps were crunching through the snow, catching up from behind. He placed a hand on Tarak's shoulder to stop him

"I'm sorry, Friend. I didn't mean that."

Tarak shrugged. "It's okay. I know."

"I don't know what's happening to me," Tuck-na-wit confided. He looked toward the lodge. It looked like a big gray and white whale beached in the snow. "Sometimes I wish I never had to go back in there ever again--that I could just go somewhere--anywhere else that death could not follow me."

Hope sparked in Tarak. Was this his chance? Maybe he would not have to leave his friend. They could go back to Wai-i-ka together. Outsiders rarely came to the high mountain village and there was no white man's disease there. He and Tuck could swim with Ghost in the Klamath every day and the sickness would never find them. Tuck-na-wit would become part of Tarak's family and they would truly be brothers.

"You would leave before Naha was sent to Memeloose?" Tarak asked, cautiously.

Tuck-na-wit shuffled silently through the snow. They were in sight of the lodge when he finally answered. "No. I couldn't do that."

Of course not, Tarak thought. Tuck needed to be here to send his mother to Memeloose, but later--afterwards, they could find Ghost and go home together.

"There is someone I would like you to meet," Tarak told Tuck-na-wit, hesitantly.

"Your woman tawati?" Tuck tried to lighten the mood.

"No. Someone else." Tuck-na-wit looked at him, waiting for him to say more, but he couldn't.

"We will talk later," he assurred is friend.

"Yes. Later," Tarak agreed.

On the fifth day, when Naha's mourning time was over, Lala dressed her mistress in her best clothes, broke the teeth from Naha's comb and melted a hole in her favorite pot, laying these prized possessions on her funeral pallet. Everything that went with Naha to the spirit world had to be made "dead", just as she was.

When the canoe bearing Naha's body slid into the river, the village women raised their voices

CHAPTER 26

in a keening cry that rode the winter wind across the cold, gray water.

Tuck-na-wit stood beside Tarak and Lala, his blanket covering all but his red, swollen eyes. Siniuse was the first to turn away, walking back to the lodge, but Lala, Tarak, and Tuck stayed until the canoe was swallowed by the island's shadow. When at last they turned to walk back to the lodge, the roof was already burning. The house that Naha had lived and died in could not be left to call her spirit back. It too must "die."

Lala cried out once then collapsed onto the beach. Losing her house as well as her mistress was more than the loyal slave woman could bear. The village women hurried to her side but pulled back quickly.

"The fever... It's the fever," they whispered. Within moments, the beach was deserted except for Tuck-na-wit, Tarak and Lala. Tuck looked down at the old slave woman.

"I am cursed."

CHAPTER TWENTY-SEVEN

Disease spread through Gulasquo village like the stink of burnt sugar salmon, whispering death at every door. Three mornings after Naha made the journey to Memeloose, Tuck-na-wit and Tarak found Lala in the snow outside the family's teepee. Confused by fever, she had crawled into the night and frozen to death.

Siniuse ordered her body dragged into the woods and abandoned. No one cared about a slave woman's spirit; a slave was not a person. Tuck-na-wit did not even argue.

Old Grandmother, Siniuse's aunt, a nephew, two cousins; the young, the old and the weak, went first, but even the strong were not spared. There was no telling where or when the disease would strike, no telling who would take to their beds and get up, weak but alive, and who would make the final journey to Memeloose.

As the death toll grew, more lodges were burned, replaced by teepees, their bright designs smeared with the soot that clung to everything like snow's dark stepsister. Desperate families began to move the sick out of their lodges before they died, so they would not have to burn them in the dead of winter. Burial traditions crumbled. There was too

CHAPTER 27

much to be done and too few left to do it. Those who were well enough to work were worn thin with trying.

Tarak and Tuck made their first canoe trip to Memeloose each morning at first light, working through the day until it was too dark to cross the water. But the line of bodies on the beach never seemed to get any shorter. There was no more talk of leaving.

"Some witch has filled my skin with rocks," Tuck-na-wit complained as he and Tarak trudged up the trail from the beach. "I can barely lift my feet and I think my arms have gone numb. How many trips did we make today?"

Tarak shook his head. "I don't know. I've stopped counting."

Tuck grunted and walked on.

A fevered moan curled through the pine trees, followed by a piercing wail. Tarak stopped, the warmth of his body escaping in the steam of his breath. All around them people were dying. Their cries ate at his insides, combing through his intestines to kill any flicker of hope that might still linger hidden there. With every breath he inhaled death. It hung on the air, and lurked in the doorways. When he closed his eyes, he saw the faces of the dead, their skin drawn tight over the bones of their faces, their lips split and blistered. The stench of unwashed, decaying bodies was in his nose and down his throat. It soured his stomach. Gulasquo village was the hunting ground for a predator that no hunter could track and no warrior could stand against.

The world, as Tarak knew it, had become unrecognizable. Was it really only three moons ago that he and Tuck-na-wit had gone to Wascopum Mission to learn the tzum tzum lines and met Hyas Tee? It seemed so much longer.

We are only children. We should not have to see and do these things. Tarak's spirit mourned the loss of an innocence he had taken for granted and been over eager to leave behind. Now it was gone and he understood why his parents had tried to hold him a little longer in their protective embrace.

A deep breath of cold air, steadied Tarak and he pushed ahead to catch up with Tuck-na-wit.

Out of the corner of his eye, he saw a lump wrapped in a blanket under a pine tree just off the trail. Two scabbed feet, blackened by frostbite, peeked out from under the frozen blanket's stiff edge.

"Ti'caw?" Tarak left the trail, pushing through the unpacked snow. "Ti'caw, it's me, Tarak." Kneeling, he touched the girl's bone-thin shoulder. It was as cold as stone.

She whimpered, clouded eyes looking through and beyond him.

"Tarak...." Slowly Ti'caw focused on his face.

"Yes, Ti'caw. It's me."

CHAPTER 27

"I'm sorry," Ti'caw forced the words out between blistered lips.

"I'm sorry too." Tarak took the blanket from around his shoulders and put it over her. "I'll get Chet'woot and we'll take you back to the village where we can get you warm--"

"No," she said firmly. "I'm not going back there; not ever. I'd rather die out here, alone."

"Don't say that," Tarak scolded her. "You're not going to die. I'm going to do like you said, Ti'caw--I'm going to ask Tuck--Chet'woot to let me go home. We can go together, just as soon as you get well."

Her peeling lips formed a pitiful smile. "It is all right for you to tell stories now, Tarak, its winter. The rattlesnakes are sleeping. They won't mind."

Tarak wanted to protest that he was not telling a story, but he knew in his heart that she was right. Ti'caw's mistress was not going to give her slave up to anything but death.

"I'm sorry about Ghost," Ti'caw added.

"What do you mean?" Tarak frowned. "What are you sorry for?"

"I lied. I did hear him that day at Silaylo Falls. I think I saw him too, later--here just before the Winter Ceremonies, after the bear attack. I think he was looking for you. I think he followed you, just like you said. He followed you all the way from Wai-i-ka, that silly dog."

Tarak sat down hard in the snow his heart and mind both racing. "Ghost was here?"

Ti'caw gave a ragged gasp. "Some men tied him up and took him away. I didn't want to believe it was him. I told myself it couldn't be him, that I was imagining it. But I wasn't. He was here, Tarak. He came for you. He is a good dog--a good friend." Ti'caw's eyes filled with tears. "No one ever loved me like that and now no one ever will. I will die here, far away from home and my spirit will wander, lost, because it can't find its way back to Wai-i-ka." Ti'caw took a sharp, raspy breath in then let it out in a long, hollow hiss. She did not breathe again.

Tarak sat in the snow as clouds, riding the cape of the night, moved in and covered the stars.

Ti'caw was dead. He wiped tears from his eyes. He knew he should tell someone, but he couldn't think who. Lala would have known what to do—or Naha, but they were both gone now. Tarak hadn't seen Big Woman in days. He didn't even know if she was still alive and after all she too was only a slave. It seemed there was no one left now but him and Tuck.

Something must have gone terribly wrong at Pik-i-owish this year, he thought. *Because the world is crumbling. Iri'waw was right. I did not understand that change and getting older are each other's shadows.*

Tarak had not been given a ceremony. He had not killed a deer, but he knew without anyone

CHAPTER 27

giving him a feather, or a feast, or a new name, that he was no longer a child. He dusted the snow off his legs and began to gather firewood.

Tuck appeared from out of the darkness. "What are you doing, Friend?"

Tarak looked at Ti'caw's body. "When a Kama'twa warrior dies far from home, their companions burn the body and bring the ashes back so their spirit can return to rest among their people and will not wander, lost. Ti'caw was from my village. You can beat me if you want, Tuck, but I will not leave her for the dogs."

Tuck-na-wit did not scold Tarak for calling him by his old boyhood name, he did not say anything. He simply began to help his friend gather wood. When they were finished they placed Ti'caw's body on the bier, lit it and watched it burn.

"Is this what it feels like to be a grown up? I don't think I like it much," Tuck-na-wit confessed. "It's too frightening. When this is over, there won't be any elders left in our village who know what to do. The old ones, with all their memories and stories, will be gone. Who will we rely on for answers? Who will know the right way to do things?" He shook his head. "There will be no one left to make things right again, only us. I don't know how to live in that world. I don't know if I want to try." Tuck-na-wit got up and stumbled through the snow to his bed.

CHAPTER TWENTY-EIGHT

The ground under Tarak's feet rose and fell in waves as he ran, his fingers clutching Ghost's fur.

"Slow down, Ghost," he called out. "Slow down!"

Ghost looked back over his shoulder, his pink tongue hanging out of the side of his mouth. His eyes became yellow, spinning whirlpools. Then suddenly, it was Coyote, not Ghost. Tarak tried to pull his hand away but it was stuck fast in the spirit animal's brown fur. They burst from the trees onto the banks of the Klamath River.

"Our son is dead," A'ni and Ata' cried from the far bank.

"No. I am not dead. I am here. I am alive," Tarak called back. But they could not hear him.

The sky opened and dirt began to rain down, burying him alive

"Stop. I am alive! I am alive!"

Tarak's eyes flew open. A patch of pale, winter sky winked beyond the smoke flap of the teepee. He breathed in the cold dawn, trying to clear his head. The smell of smoke from Ti'caw's funeral pyre still clung to his shirt, his skin, his hair.

CHAPTER 28

"Wake up, Tuck," he said, hoarsely. "It's light. We need to get to work." In spite of the cold, Tuck-na-wit had thrown off his hide coverings. Tarak reached over to jostle his friend's shoulder.

"Tuck?" He pulled his hand away. The heat from Tuck-na-wit's body was like the hot stones in a Sweat House. "No. Not Tuck. Please, not Tuck," Tarak whispered. He turned to call for help then stopped. Who would come? Siniuse's bed was empty and the last servant woman left in the household was nowhere to be seen.

Tarak went to the door and pulled back the flap. Siniuse's tracks led toward Tot's.

The leather bundle holding Ti'caw's ashes lay in the snow beside the door where he had dropped it last night before stumbling to bed.

"This is your chance," her voice whispered inside his head. *"Leave now. No one will even notice you're gone until night. Maybe not even then."*

The bear claw necklace on Tuck-na-wit's chest moved up and down as he breathed. If Tarak left now, what would happen to Tuck? Not many survived the fever but some did. Tuck-na-wit could be one of them.

"He is young and strong. He can make it through this," Tarak said, firmly.

"Don't be a fool," Ti'caw's spirit sneered. *"He is dead already."*

"No, he is not."

"Forget about him! He calls you his slave."

Tarak wavered, thinking about home, finding Ghost...all the things he still wished for his own life.

"That's right, Tarak." Ti'caw's spirit wheezed. *"Think about yourself. Other people don't care. Their affections are fleeting; their promises meaningless."*

"Maybe. But mine are not," Tarak decided.

"You? Who are you? You're a slave boy, a nothing; no one."

"Stop, Ti'caw. I am not listening to you anymore. You do not understand." Tarak stepped out of the teepee and into Siniuse's tracks.

"You owe him nothing!" the girl's spirit screamed.

"Friendship is not measured by what you owe, Ti'caw. It is measured by what you give. I am sorry you could not learn that before you died."

Tot looked up and nodded in greeting as Tarak entered the lodge.

"If my son wants breakfast, tell him to find that lazy slave woman," Siniuse said gruffly, not looking up from his own meal.

"This is not about breakfast," Tarak answered. "It is about your son. You should come. He has the fever."

Siniuse looked up, staring at Tarak as if he had spoken some strange language.

"He has not been sick long though, right?" Tot jumped in. "He was fine yesterday."

CHAPTER 28

"Yes." Tarak nodded. "Yesterday, he was fine." A shiver of dread passed through Tarak as he remembered Tuck's words about not wanting to live in this world anymore.

Tot turned to Siniuse. "The weather has cleared, brother. I will go upriver and bring Konaway Se'ahost back." Tot began to gather the things he would need for the trip.

"Please hurry, Uncle," Tarak urged him.

Siniuse stood and slapped Tarak across the face.

"He is not your uncle!" He pushed Tarak aside as he ran from the lodge.

Tot put a reassuring hand on Tarak's shoulder. "Don't mind him, Friend. Grief has taken his mind. I don't know what he will do if he loses Chet'woot, too. You did the right thing though, coming to tell us. I thank you. I know you will look after my nephew and his father. I will return with Se'ahost as soon as I can."

When Tarak returned to the tepee, Siniuse was sitting beside his son's bed, holding the red pasessee Tuck-na-wit had given Naha. He had been secretly sleeping with it bundled against him, under the hides, ever since she had died.

The grieving man turned violently and threw the shawl onto the fire's coals. "Will they leave us nothing, these white devils?" he shouted, before storming out.

Tarak built up the fire and made some acorn mush. He found an empty leather bag and began filling it with travel food, a knife... anything he and Tuck and Ghost might need to travel south, stashing it all in a bundle behind the stacks of storage baskets. When he was done, he poured water onto a piece of old, worn blanket and began to gently dab Tuck-na-wit's forehead and cheeks, trying to pull the fever from his body.

"Stay with me, Tuck. Get well then we will find Ghost and go home, where there is no fever, and the air does not stink of death. Do not give up. I know it is hard, and it seems hopeless sometimes, but the old ones faced challenges in their lives and they never gave up. Where would we be if they had not? We live because of their strength and that strength lives on in us. Together, we can make things good again, you, and I, and Ghost. I know we can. We have to, because it is our world now."

Tuck-na-wit opened his eyes and looked up at Tarak.

"You are my best and truest brother; not a slave," he said in a hoarse voice. "You understand? I free you. You are not a slave anymore. I give you what should not have been taken from you except that I was so lonely. Our brotherhood filled that loneliness. You saved me long before you threw rocks at the stupid bear." He tried to smile. "Lemolo siwash." He closed his eyes, sighing.

"Mahsie. I am proud to be called Chet'woot's brother." Tarak pulled the feather Kamiakin had given him out from under his shirt

CHAPTER 28

and tied it into his dark hair. He had earned his place among the tillikum.

*****

When Tarak opened his eyes again it was dark. He had stayed beside Tuck-na-wit all day, finally falling asleep slumped forward onto the bed, but now voices outside had awoken him.

"I do not work on the white men, Siniuse. You know this. I hold to the old ways, so my tamanawas is whole and unbroken. I can banish these bad spirits from Chet'woot."

"Proud words, Se'ahost. See they are not too proud," Siniuse's deep voice carried through the teepee walls. "For I too hold to the old ways. Save my son's life and I will give you whatever you ask but fail and, by the old laws, I will demand your life."

CHAPTER TWENTY-NINE

Tarak melted into the shadows at the far end of the teepee, afraid to stay, afraid to leave. What would the tawati do to Tuck-na-wit? Would he be able to keep his promise to Siniuse and send the sickness away? Did he have such power? Tarak was not sure. Se'ahost was not respected as a man of wisdom. Though he gave out healing herbs and did ceremonies for the sick, he was petty and vindictive; a man, like any other man, with some knowledge but many faults. The power to heal belonged to the Spirit's, not men. Could Se'ahost, call the spirits and be granted what he requested?

The tawati set his medicine bundle on the floor near the teepee's fire, mumbling sing-song words as he set out an abalone shell, a pipe, six pa-tash sticks with carved faces, a large, wooden bowl, and the topknots and tails of birds and animals of power. Chanting quietly, he chose a rock and began to pound the pa-tash sticks into the ground making a circle. He emptied the last of the water in the waterskin by the door into the wooden bowl then took coals from the fire, sprinkling silver fir needles onto their hot surface. A smoky perfume filled the teepee. Men from the village arrived, carrying hollow wooden drums and settled

CHAPTER 29

themselves into a second circle of six on the outside of the pa'tash sticks.

"You." Se'ahost pointed at Tarak. "Chet'woot's Friend. Sit in the middle." Tarak stood, rolled back his shoulders and pushed down the fear fluttering in his stomach. All eyes watched him as he walked to the center of the double circle. The carved faces of the pa'tash sticks seemed to follow him even through their closed lids, each stick with a different face. Tarak could sense spirit within them and he swallowed hard, clasping his hands together so no one would see how they shook.

Se'ahost removed the hide coverings from Tuck-na-wit. The bitter sadness of Ti'caw's funeral pyre wafted through the air. The tawati leaned over and sniffed the scent. His eyes sought Tarak's. He knew what they had done in the woods last night. He filled his pipe and sat to smoke it with the drummers.

Tarak sat, trembling, alone in the center of the circle,

"You should have left when I told you to," Ti'caw's dead voice whispered.

"I could not," Tarak repeated firmly. *"He is my friend."* Ti'caw's mocking laugh danced around the room and out into the tree tops.

When the tawati's pipe was empty, Se'ahost stood and drew his arms above his head, beginning the first prayer song. Slowly, the men began to beat out a steady rhythm on their drums.

The pace picked up, vibrating off the teepee walls until the sound was so dense Tarak felt he could touch it, taste it, take it into him and wrap it around him.

The carved eyes on the pa'tash sticks flew open, bright as coals in their shadowy faces. One at a time, they spun loose from their stations in the ground, jumping up and down as they joined the dance of the drums.

Se'ahost turned again to Tarak.

"Take hold." He pointed to one of the sticks. Tarak froze. "If you truly wish the sickness to leave your master's body then dance with the spirits and tell them so."

"I do." Tarak reached out and took hold of the nearest stick. Power shot up his arm and through his body like he had grabbed a lightning bolt. Frightened, he tried to let go, but he could not. The stick stuck with him as if it had been sewn to his skin.

Se'ahost chuckled. "Pray hard, little slave. Pray that your master lives--if that is what you really want."

Tarak did want it. No matter what the old tawati said, he was Tuck-na-wit's friend.

"Help his heart find peace, Spirits. Please. Please, remove this despair and make him strong again." The stick danced Tarak up and down, its power and his prayer coming together until each was the other and both were one.

CHAPTER 29

The drums played on and Tarak danced deep into the night while Se'ahost sniffed at Tuck-na-wit's body, sucking up the illness he found there and spitting it out into the bowl of water. As the moon climbed into the sky then sank down again, the drummers took turns drumming and resting, but there was no rest for Se'ahost or Tarak, who walked in the spirit world.

Tarak and Ghost were walking along the upper Klamath River when they came across Chiwa'chni and Ti'caw giggling together on the riverbank, their fingers and lips stained red with berry juice.

"I am looking for Tuck-na-wit. Have you seen him?" Tarak asked.

"He is not here yet." Ti'caw popped a ripe berry into her mouth. "I think he is coming soon though."

Tarak thought about this. "If he comes, will he be dead?"

"Yes."

"Then I don't want him to come. I don't want him to die."

Ti'caw shrugged. "You cannot do anything about it. You are just a slave boy."

"No, I am not--not anymore. Tuck-na-wit freed me."

"Really? Was anyone else there to hear?" Ti'caw challenged him. Tarak did not answer. "You are still a fool, Tarak. Siniuse will never let you go," she warned him.

"I do not belong to Siniuse. I belonged to Tuck-na-wit and he gave me my freedom. I am his brother now--not a slave."

"A dead man's gift. It means nothing." Ti'caw shook her head, resuming eating berries.

*****

Tarak woke on the floor of the teepee. The drums had stopped and a wintery dawn splashed sunlight across the threshold. All signs of the night's ceremony had been completely swept away. Glancing at Tuck-na-wit's bed, Tarak moved quietly to the teepee door and stepped out into the bright cold. Konaway Se'ahost stood before Siniuse.

"There is nothing more to do," the tawati said, his face drawn from the strain of the long night's work. "No tamanawas can bring a person's spirit back to their body if they do not want to return--no matter how powerful their tah is."

Siniuse's eyes blazed, his hands clenched in rage. "You knew the price for failure, Se'ahost. You accepted."

The tawati raised his chin, trying to match the taller man's height. "The failure is not mine, Siniuse. It is yours. Chet'woot's spirit no longer wants to live here. Why is that? He is young. He should be full of hope. Instead, his spirit is sad and frightened, and bitter with regret and loss. This is not my doing. It is his father's."

CHAPTER 29

"Look around," Siniuse growled. "Do you see hope here? We are being wiped off our own lands--everything we are, everything we have, taken from us. It was not me who sent hope away."

"That is the world you see--the world you chose to show your son. Now you pay the price for it." Se'ahost pointed his finger at Siniuse's face. "When your oldest son died, you crawled inside yourself and turned your heart to stone. Your house filled with darkness and you welcomed it. Now this darkness sucks everything from your life. I removed the sickness from Chet'woot's body but I cannot remove the sickness from his spirit. It sees no light here among us and refuses to return."

"Then make it return!" Siniuse shouted, his face red. "He is all I have left--my last son. Make him want to live!"

Se'ahost shook his head. "Only you could have done that and you did not." The tawati walked away through the snowy landscape.

Tarak felt as if a deep, dark hole had opened up at his feet and if he moved one step he would slide into it.

Siniuse turned to Tot, a cold light in his eyes. "If my son dies, Konaway Se'ahost follows him to Memeloose. It is my right."

Tot placed a calming hand on his brother-in-law's shoulder. "Chet'woot is not dead yet, brother. If this is a white man's disease, maybe it takes a white man to cure it. Let go of your pride and send to the fort for the white doctin. Save your son."

Tarak felt Siniuse's icy gaze turn to him like a predator focusing in on its prey.

"Slave boy. Mamook Klatawa. Go. Mamook chako. Bring back the white doctin with his la metsin. Alta!"

Hope drove its heels hard into Tarak's sides.

"Nawitka." He took off with the speed of an arrow released from a bow. Pushing a canoe into the river, he headed downstream for Fort Vancouver.

CHAPTER THIRTY

The moon was high when Tarak came to the rapids at Wy-wy-eke. The portage path around the wild stretch of water was wide and well traveled for good reason. Those who ignored it came to regret it. Many of the American settlers, unable to portage their large log rafts around the rapids, lost all their worldly possessions and sometimes their lives to the legendary stretch of wild water. But when Siniuse had ordered Tarak to fetch the white doctor from Fort Vancouver, none of this had been in Tarak's mind. Only later, when the adrenaline had left him tired and drained and his stomach began to growl did he realize that he had packed no food, nothing to trade, and brought no one to help him in any way.

Tarak stretched his legs, rubbing out the numbness from long hours of keeping them folded under him. He rolled his arms and neck to relieve the stiffness then checked the knot on Kamiakin's feather tied in his hair.

The rapids ahead sounded like a trampling herd.

"Great River, it is me, Tarak," he said respectfully. "I know you are powerful and dangerous, but you are also generous. You give the tillikum along your shores everything they need to live. Please, look into my heart and see that though I am just a foolish boy. I do not come here to prove something, or to brag. I come because I wish to help my friend. I danced with the Patash people, now I beg you; let me pass so Chet'woot can live."

Tarak raised his head, gathered the last threads of his resolve and searched the silver tipped ripples of the fast moving water for the arrow point that would mark the deepest channel through the rapids. Ripples curved together, forming the tzum tzum line "v". Tarak directed the canoe's bow toward the spot and braced his feet.

The water bucked and tossed canoe and rider up into the air then dropped them down into a watery canyon. The spray hung suspended like a million tiny stars, glowing against the dark night. A wave stretched tall overhead, curled and broke over Tarak's head and shoulders, drenching him in ice cold water. He shook the water from his eyes and went on; shifting his paddle from side to side, digging it in deep; always moving forward.

He fended off rocks, leaning his weight back when the canoe dove low, digging, sweeping, maneuvering past boulders, and through fast moving channels. There was no room in his mind for anything but the canoe, the river, and the point where the two met. Then subtly, magically, something shifted within Tarak and he realized that he and the river were not challengers pitted against

CHAPTER 30

each other, they were joyful companions traveling the same path; relishing the journey they shared.

Tarak sensed the playfulness beneath the water's power and its deep love of its own wild nature. It was not trying to drown him; it was inviting him to join its majestic romp to the sea.

The tight ball inside Tarak's chest relaxed and for the first time in weeks, laughter bubbled up inside him, the sound bouncing off the cliffs and echoing across the water.

"Hiyea!" he shouted, as the canoe shot forward with a new eagerness and ease.

Death and sadness fell behind. The guilt of poor choices, the frustration of being powerless and the disappointment of all his lost dreams, sieved away. Once again Tarak felt filled with the power of youth. He was a part of everything and everything was a part of him. The strength of a million living relatives from the tiniest insect to the farthest stars in the sky raced through him. He could do anything.

The river current slowed, becoming a smooth surface of glassy, circles, kissed by moonlight. Tarak turned and looked back upstream. Wy-wy-eke was behind him.

I made it! he realized. "Hiyea! I made it!" He faced downstream. From here to the Pacific Ocean, the Great River would be wide and flat, its strength hidden in deep channels. Kamiakin's feather fluttered in Tarak's hair, tickling his cheek and gratitude filled his heart. He was free and alive; everything seemed possible again.

"Thank you," he said softly to the river. "I will fetch the doctin and he will save my brother then I will find Ghost, and we will go home."

*****

The sun was high when Tarak climbed the bank to Kanaka village. Men with white skin, brown skin, red, yellow, and shades that were almost black walked the narrow, muddy streets, and in and out of the shops that lined them.

"Mamook elan! Ticky metsin man," Tarak's voice folded into the dough of the busy village's rattle and clang.

"Na cheechako," he approached a man, politely. "Klah howyum."

"Out of my way, brat." The man pushed him, tumbling Tarak into the mud. The boy's face flushed hot and his fists' clenched as the man walked away through the crowd.

"Coyote loves to play tricks on those that think they are important." Iri'wa's voice played inside Tarak's head. *"Do you think you are important, Tarak?"*

"No," Tarak answered silently. *"Getting the doctin for Tuck-na-wit is what is important. No one will drive me from that path."* He wiped his hands on his buckskin leggings and stood. "Please help me find men of good heart here," he muttered

CHAPTER 30

under his breath. Kamiakin had said such men and women could be found among all peoples. Tarak hoped it was true. Standing in the middle of the street, Tarak closed his eyes, and reached out with his spirit into the everything.

"Open their ears. Open their hearts, and let them hear my need and help me."

People continued to stream by him like water going around a boulder, as if he were invisible then a tall man with red hair, stopped.

"Are you all right there, laddie?" Angus McDonald asked.

Tarak opened his eyes. "Mamook elann. Ticky doctin. Ticky metsin man." he said humbly, his eyes glistening with unshed tears.

The Scotsman took the boy's measure then pointed to a gate in the stockade wall. "Doc Gairdner is in there. Ask at the wee door. Tell 'em Angus McDonald sent you."

"Mahsie." Tarak sprinted to the stockade wall. Pounding his fists against the gatehouse door he shouted, "Mamook elan! Ticky metsin man."

A short door, chest high above the ground, swung open on iron hinges.

"Kah, tenas tillikum? What you want boy?" the whiskered gateman asked in the heavy accent of a King Georgeman.

Tarak repeated his request.

The man shook his gray head. "No siwash inside the Fort walls 'less you're an employee or a guest on official business. Kumptus? Ya' got to be invited to come inside." He shut the door.

Tarak was still staring at it and trying to remember the red haired man's odd name when the lilt of silver bells came tumbling above the noise of the street.

He turned as the crowd parted, revealing Hyas Tee and Marguerite McLoughlin. The white-maned man sat high on his spotted horse, his long black coat and high beaver hat making him look even taller than the six feet four inches nature had given him. Marguerite, the skirt of her blue velvet riding dress spread out across the dappled rump of her new Appaloosa horse, was his opposite; short and matronly with flesh softened features plumping out her handsome face.

As the big gate swung open to let the territory's "royal couple" pass inside, Tarak dodged around to the front of the horses, promptly colliding with someone hurrying out of the gate.

Sitting in the mud, Tarak looked up into the surprised face of Jimmy Buckeye.

"Jimmy? Jimmy! Nah sikhs!" A smile blossomed on Tarak's face.

"Nah sikhs to you cheechako." Jimmy grinned back, rubbing his head. "You're a long way from home aren't you, little brother?" he switched from the jargon into the language of the Takelma as he rose, brushing clumps of mud from his britches.

CHAPTER 30

"I've come to ask Hyas Tee to send the white doctin to my village to work his la metsin."

"Hold on, cheechako. Slow down. Doc Gairdner can't be going all the way to Wai-i-ka. He's got plenty of sick folk right here to take care of."

"No, I don't mean to Wai-i-ka, Jimmy. I came from Gulasquo village, upriver," Tarak corrected the young trapper.

Jimmy looked puzzled.

"Tenas tillikum nawitka, Mister Buckeye?" Marguerite McLoughlin leaned from her saddle, peeking around to see if anyone had been hurt in the mishap.

"Jimmy, you know this boy?" Hyas Tee asked from his tall horse. Jimmy removed his hat and acknowledged both the McLoughlins.

"Nawitka, Hyas Tee. Ma'am."

"Mamook elan." Tarak turned to the man the tillikum called The Great White Eagle then to his wife, pleading for their help. McLoughlin eyed him carefully.

"This is one of the boys we fished out of the river last fall, isn't it, John?" Marguerite's dark eyes missed little. The daughter of a chief man among the elders of his village, she was keenly aware of her unique station and importance in the territory, and though her influence remained subtle, it was also firm, particularly when it came to children.

"I believe you are right, my dear," Hyas Tee replied.

Jimmy looked even more confused. "What are you doing here?" he asked Tarak.

"It is a long story," Tarak said, his eyes welling up against his will.

"John?" Marguerite's eyes made a silent request.

"Bring the boy inside, Jimmy," Dr McLoughlin's deep voice commanded. "We can certainly sort this out someplace other than the street, kumptus?"

Jimmy followed the two riders into the fort, leading Tarak through the gate and across the open green.

Handing off their horses to a groom, the McLoughlins waited on the porch of the trim clapboard house that served as the Chief Factor's residence. A company clerk and the red haired Scot, Angus McDonald, joined them.

"So where do you know this lad from, Jimmy?" McLoughlin asked as he checked over the ledger the clerk handed him.

"We met in his village last summer, below the big white mountain called Wai-i-ka when Loo-ee and I were trapping there."

McLoughlin raised a bushy eyebrow. "That is a long way from where we found him drowning in the Great River last fall."

"Klahowyum, Hyas Tee," Tarak pleaded again. "Please give mercy. My friend needs la

CHAPTER 30

metsin. You remember Tuck-na-wit; Siniuse's son? Ticky shama doctin. He's very sick." The jargon was a language of trade. If there were words of emotion, Tarak did not know them, but he was sure that if there had ever been a man of great heart among these white people, this was him. Tarak tried to will the tall man's pale eyes to look into his own heart and understand what his words could not say.

"Tuck-na-wit." Angus scratched his chin. "That'd be the Gulasquo lad folks been talkin' aboot? The one who killed a bear the day the volcanoe erupted?"

"The same boy who we rescued from the river last fall--along with his slave." McLoughlin indicated Tarak.

Jimmy Buckeye's confusion became a frown and he turned to Tarak.

"I don't understand. Hyas Tee says he saved you from drowning in the Great River in The Moon of Falling Leaves and that you are the slave of some boy called Tuck-na-wit."

Tarak could feel the blood rise to his cheeks.

"The day after you and Loo-ee left, the Snake raided our village," he muttered. Why was it so hard to say it? It was not as if it was his fault he had been captured. "They brought us to Silaylo Falls and sold me to Tuck-na-wit's father."

Jimmy's face clouded over. He turned to McLoughlin, speaking quickly in the white man's wawa.

Angus McDonald studied Tarak, his eyes lighting on the feather in his hair.

"You know Kamiakin?" he said softly so only the boy would hear.

Tarak's eyes went wide.

"Kamiakin nika khapo; he is my brother. "He told me of meeting the boy who saved his brother from a bear." He smiled and stretched out his hand in the white man's gesture of friendship."It is an honor, young man."

Tarak hesitantly took the man's hand, remembering what Reverend Perkins had said about the white man's custom.

When McLoughlin turned his attention back to them, he was wearing Jimmy's frown.

"You came all the way down river, alone, to get a doctor to save your master?" he muttered. "He could have just run away."

Marguerite placed a gentle hand on Mcloughlin's arm. "The boy asks for our help, husband. Surely there is something we can do?"

Dr McLoughlin hesitated no more. "Jimmy, have some of the men get a le boat ready to go upriver, and fetch Doc Gairdner. If they hurry, they can catch the incoming tide."

Tarak took a deep breath. "Mahsie, Hyas Tee."

CHAPTER 30

A half hour later, Jimmy, Angus and Tarak were following Doc Gairdner to the beach.

"You should not go back, cheechako," Jimmy warned Tarak. "It is not necessary. Send the doctor but stay here with Loo-ee and me."

Tarak shook his head. "I can't do that, Jimmy. Tuck needs me."

"For what? You are not a doctor. I know you want to help your friend but you've done what you could for him; you got the doctor to go upriver. There is nothing more you can do. Look, when we go trapping in the spring you can go with us, or we will take you back home, but do not go back to that place, Tarak. It is dangerous."

Home: the word trickled over Tarak's ears like cool water. How many times had he imagined finding Jimmy and having him say these words to him? But those had been the fantasies of a child. In the real world things were not that simple.

"It is very kind of you to offer to help someone who is really no more than a stranger to you, Jimmy, but you don't understand. I have to go," he said, firmly.

"Then I will go with you," Jimmy announced, his face as dark as a thundercloud.

"A very bad idea, Jimmy lad. If the fever has killed so many, those who are not sick in their beds will be frightened and angry and lookin' to blame someone. You show up, uninvited, with your dander all up, and there could be trouble."

"I can handle trouble," Jimmy argued.

Angus raised an eyebrow. "Maybe, maybe not but there is more to this than your sense of injustice, my friend. There is the peace along the river to consider. It only takes one man to slit your throat, or shoot an arrow into you. If things turn bad, it will be more than your own hands tha' get burned, Jimmy lad. The whole region could go up like a keg o' powder." Angus shook his head.

"If it's not safe for me, it can't be safe for Tarak," Jimmy grumbled after a few minutes. "You're just being stubborn, for no good reason Tarak

"There is a reason," Tarak replied. "There's Ghost."

Jimmy stopped like he'd run into a wall.
"Ghost?"

"You remember my dog, Ghost, don't you? He followed us when the snake took us. He's here on the Great River. I can't go back without him and the only place he knows to look for me is Gulasquo."

Jimmy stared at Tarak. "How do you know this?"

"Someone saw him being taken away from the village by some white men last fall, just after we were attacked by the bear. He was there then, when the bear attacked. I saw him, but he got hurt and I was sick in bed so…" Tarak let the words drift off. "Don't you see? He'll come back. And when he does, I need to be there.

CHAPTER 30

Jimmy's eyes took on a far away gaze as he looked out at the Great River. "Ghost, of course I remember him. I don't know where he is now, cheechako, but a few weeks ago he was here at Fort Vancouver. That would have been just before the Winter Ceremonies."

Angus gave Jimmy a stern look. "Are you two talkin' aboot the same dog; Skookum?"

Jimmy nodded. "That's the one. But that was not the first time I saw him after we left Wai-i-ka." He cleared his throat. "He traveled with Loo-ee and I when we came north last fall."

Tarak stood rooted in place, unable to catch his breath.

"We were five days from Wai-i-ka when we found him lying in the middle of the trail. He had an arrow wound in his side," Jimmy explained. "And he was bad off. Loo-ee and me patched him up, fed him, and took him along with us. We couldn't just leave him there to die, right? So he went with us. He was with us all the way to Silaylo Falls."

"The last fish run," Angus muttered.

"When I was sold," Tarak added.

"Yes." The party began to move again. "One day, there at the falls, Ghost started carrying on, barking. I didn't know what had gotten into him but he wouldn't settle down. Then all of a sudden, he just pulled free and took off running downriver."

"He was trying to get to me." *And he made it*, Tarak thought. *On the day the bear attacked.* "Tuck-na-wit's arrow shot the bear in the eye but it was Ghost who saved us. He drew the bear away from us and fought it so we could get to safety."

"And you just left him out there?" Jimmy demanded.

"I didn't know." Tarak's eyes spilled over with tears. "The bear had clawed me. I was wounded and I wasn't sure what I'd seen--if it was real or not. I was hurt and out of my head. Once I got well, I went back to look for him, but there was nothing left, no tracks – nothing. It had been too long. Then a few days ago, a friend told me she'd seen him being taken away."

Jimmy was trying hard to put the pieces together. "After Silaylo, I didn't see him until a few weeks ago when he showed up here in some trader's cage. I'd just convinced the old skinflint the dog was mine when Angus let Ghost out of the cage and he bolted. I asked around. People who saw him, said that he was headed upriver."

Angus, Jimmy, and Tarak stopped at the shore. The le boat with Doc Gairdner and six strong sturdy Voyageurs was waiting for them.

"The beastie's still lookin' for you, lad," Angus said.

"I have to get back." Tarak climbed in and the voyageurs pushed out into the water.

CHAPTER 30

"When you find him, you both come back here, kumptus?" Jimmy called after him. "Loo-ee and I will be watching for you."

Jimmy and Angus watched from the beach as the company started upriver.

"Do you think Ghost will find him?" Jimmy asked, watching the voyageurs pull the le boat up river.

Angus laughed. "I would'na be bettin' against that dog, Jimmy. I think you'd lose."

*****

The stink from the dying village tainted the air well downriver. Gulasquo had become a charred skeleton of its old self. Of those not dead or bedridden, a third sat studying the smoke curling through the grey skies, while another third spent their day watching the snow melt. Tarak caught a glimpse of Se'ahost skulking among the trees just outside the village.

So you are not dead yet eh, old tawati? he thought.

The coming of the white doctin was a slap in the face to the old healer, stripping him of any respect he still held within the village.

Word had been passed to Siniuse that a le boat was coming and he stood outside his teepee, his arms folded across his chest, glaring as if daring them to approach.

"Doctin." Gairdner pointed to himself. "La metsin." He held up his black bag. "Tuck-na-wit?"

Siniuse's eyes narrowed. "No Tuck-na-wit: Chet'woot. My son is a man now."

"Chet'woot, kumptus." Gairdner corrected himself, waiting to be taken to his patient.

For a moment Tarak thought Siniuse would refuse to let the white man in but at last he stepped aside and opened the flap.

Too soon, the doctor returned.

"I'm sorry." Gairdner shook his head. "You called me too late. There is nothing I can do. You understand? It is ended; kaput. Maybe, if you had sent for me before..." His eyes took in the ruined village. "But now, there is nothing I can do," he repeated softly. Tuck-na-wit was dead.

CHAPTER THIRTY-ONE

Silence clung to Siniuse's teepee like a spider's dark web. There were no women left in the household to mourn. The last slave woman had finally been sent away to help in Tot's longhouse. Siniuse's birdlike profile was a carved totem keeping vigil beside his son's body. He did not scowl at Tarak when his son's friend tip-toed by, or notice when Tarak put food in front of him, or when he quietly tended the fire. He did not mark Tarak's coming and going at all. His spirit had forgotten that it had a body.

Tarak's head and chest felt tight and heavy, as if something too big to fit there was swelling inside him. Tuck-na-wit was gone and he would not return. Once again, Tarak faced how alone he was here. He slipped quietly from the teepee and checked the pack he had stashed in the bushes, taking stock: travel food, a heavy wool blanket, a hide, a knife, a bow with a quiver and a dozen arrows. It was all there. He tucked the small leather bag containing Ti'caw's ashes in under the rest, added a whetstone, a pair of Tuck-na-wit's tall winter moccasins, and more sugar salmon then re-wrapped everything and pushed it far back under the tangle of brush.

He was ready. All he needed was for Ghost to come.

"Hurry, Old Bear. I am waiting," Tarak whispered to the wind, hoping it would carry his words to his friend.

Bone weary, he returned to the teepee, burrowed into a pile of blankets and fell into an exhausted sleep.

When he woke, the sunset glowed low on the teepee's west wall.

"*I must have rolled near the fire,*" he thought, his forehead and cheeks burning. "*It is late; time for dinner. Tuck-na-wit will want....* No, Tarak remembered; Tuck-na-wit would not want anything anymore. Sadness closed on Tarak's heart like a tight fist. Covering his face with his arm, he closed his eyes and drifted back into an uneasy sleep.

In his dream Iri'wa, Chiwa'chni, Ti'caw, Ghost, and Coyote were circling around him, shooting words at him like arrows.

"I don't understand. What are you trying to tell me?" he cried, unable to hear their answer.

The dream played over and over again. "Stop! Please stop!" he begged, but they did not.

The sound of his own teeth chattering woke Tarak. *Siniuse must have thrown me out in the snow, like Lala,* he thought. But the pile of blankets still cocooned him. He wriggled deeper into their dark cave, desperate for warmth.

CHAPTER 31

The third time Tarak woke, it was light outside again. He rubbed his eyes, peering out from under the blankets.

Big Woman and Tuck-na-wit's aunties were finishing preparing Tuck's body for burial. Tarak had slept through the last three days of mourning. He sat up; dizzy and weak from hunger, letting the blankets that had covered him fall away.

Big Woman saw him and her eyes blinked, looking again, as if not trusting what she was seeing. She glanced nervously toward the other women and gave Tarak a silent warning.

"Don't move. Be quiet," she motioned him in quick finger signs.

Dressed in his best clothes, Tuck-na-wit had been placed on a cedar pallet. His new bow, quiver and arrows had been broken and set carefully beside him. His bear claw necklace lay on his chest, the sinew string cut. Tot's wife tucked her nephew's medicine bundle under his arm, sliced a hole in the wool blanket that would be used to cover him to "kill" it, so he would have the use of it in the other world then covered him with it.

"It is done," she declared. The women filed out. Only Big Woman held back.

"What are you doing here, Tarak?" she hissed. "We thought you were gone."

"No. I was here. I was just sleeping." Tarak rubbed his eyes.

"For three days?"

Tarak shrugged. "I was tired. Maybe I was sick."

"It doesn't matter. You have to go, now," Big Woman insisted, glancing fearfully over her shoulder at the door. "They cannot find you here. Hurry, before they come in." Big Woman reached down and pulled Tarak from the blankets, pushing him toward the teepee's wall. "Hide in the woods. I will find you."

"But I--"

"There is no time, Tarak! If they see you, they will take you too."

"Take me where, Big Woman?" Tarak asked, dully.

"To Memeloose--to the House of the Dead--to the Bone Turner!"

Steps were approaching outside. Giving Tarak a final push, Big Woman sailed across the teepee. Blocking the doorway with her large frame, she covered her face with her hands and began to wail loudly.

"Out of the way, slave," Siniuse's gruff voice commanded. Half a dozen men poured in through the door with Siniuse coming in last. His eyes adjusted to the dark and lit on Tarak.

"So you did not run away after all, eh, slave?" He reached out and ripped the feather from Tarak's hair. "Who did you steal this from?" he hissed. A hank of Tarak's hair clung to the sinew ties.

CHAPTER 31

Ignoring the sting of his scalp, Tarak pulled himself up to his full height.

"I did not steal anything. Kamiakin of the Kikiya gave it to me at the Winter Ceremonies on the night my brother was named Chet'woot."

Siniuse slapped Tarak across the face. "Do not ever speak my son's name again. You disgrace my family with your lies. You are not worthy of the friendship he gave you, slave."

Tarak's chin went up. "You speak wrongly, Uncle. I am no slave. Before he died, my brother freed me."

Siniuse's eyes burned like dark coals. "You are a liar," he growled. "Take him."

The warriors glanced at each other. If Chet'woot had freed Tarak then Tarak was a human being now, a member of their village with all the same rights and privileges. Tarak had saved Chet'woot's life. The family owed him a debt; everyone knew it. It would have been honorable for Tuck-na-wit to repay it before he died.

"I said take him!" Siniuse roared, his rage filling the teepee. Abandoning the voices of their consciences, the men fanned out to surround Tarak.

With one swift movement, Tarak pulled his knife from its sheath, slit the back wall of the tent and leapt into the snow bank on the other side.

"Do not let him get away!"

Bloodcurdling whoops swept across the cold, gray sky as the men spilled from the tent. Whatever their misgivings, the chase was on.

Adrenaline gave Tarak's legs strength. He reached the path to the forest and sprinted up the hill.

Following the packed trail was easier than wading through the powdery snow but there was no hiding. His tracks were clear, and the further he got from the village, the deeper the snow became. He broke through the thin top crust and sank knee deep into the white powder. The only places not covered in snow were the circles of bare ground under the skirted pines. Tarak dove in under the branches. Running from tree to tree in a crouch, staying on the downwind side where the trees had provided the most shelter, he ran. On the far side, he left the cover of the pines, leaping from log to log then log to rock--choosing any firm surface that would keep him out of the snow. But the strength that fear had loaned him was burning away quickly.

Tarak stopped to catch his breath. The men were stretched out in a line between him and the village, moving toward him.

Where can I hide? Tarak thought, frantically. The cliff face where he and Tuck had run to escape the bear towered above him. He scrambled to it and began to climb as his mind returned to the past seeing, Tuck-na-wit climbing up and sliding back on the scree, the bear's jaws opening in front of him and Ghost challenging the bear half-seen behind a curtain of falling ash.

CHAPTER 31

Sobs shredded Tarak's breath and tears blurred his eyes.

He was half way up the shale slide when the village men lifted him off the ground, arms and legs kicking.

"I am not a slave. I am a free human being," he shouted. "Tuck-na-wit freed me. Listen to me. I am a human being!" But it was as if they had plugged up their ears and could not hear him.

The men carried Tarak back to Siniuse's teepee, bound his hands behind his back and put him on Tuck-na-wit's burial pallet, tying him face to face, nose to nose, and belly to belly with Tuck-na-wit's dead body.

Hope left like a flood breaking a dam. He was not Tuck-na-wit's brother. He was not his friend. He was just something Tuck-na-wit had owned, like his favorite bow.

The men lifted the pallet to their shoulders and carried it to a canoe waiting on the beach.

"What are you doing, evil siwashes? This is cultus!" Big Woman pounded her fists against their backs, trying to break through to Tarak. "Mamook kalapi; turn around! You know this boy. He is a good boy." She turned and shrieked at the few villagers who had gathered on the bank to watch the drama. "He was Chet'woot's friend! He saved his life! He is a human being."

The men pushed her back. The villagers ignored her.

"Elan mamook! He's just a tenas tillikum--just a boy. Stop this!" she begged. But no one did.

"Big Woman, watch for Ghost," Tarak out called to her. "Do you hear me?"

"Yes, I hear you, Tarak."

"He is coming. He will be here. I don't know how long it will take him, but he will come. Take care of him for me. Don't let them hurt him. He is a good dog."

"I am so sorry, Tarak." Big Woman wrung her hands. "I am so sorry. Forgive me."

Tarak began his old chant: *"I am a stone and stones do not cry."* He was going to Memeloose and nothing could stop that now, but he could choose to go bravely. *"I will not show my enemy weakness,"* he promised himself.

The men lay the burial pallet in the bottom of the canoe, settled themselves, and with long strokes, pushed it out into the water, heading for the Island of the Dead.

CHAPTER THIRTY-TWO

In the cold days of winter, the journey from Fort Vancouver to Gulasquo village was a long and bitter one for Ghost. Sharp winds scoured the gorge, hurling themselves against the high bluffs like spoiled children in the throes of a tantrum. Icy fingers needled through Ghost's fur, chilling him to the bone. It snowed and white flakes twirled down from heavy clouds. It rained, and the low, gray, sky seemed to be draped between the trees, heavy and wet.

One night, what began as rain in the sky, fell to a world so cold that the raindrops froze wherever they touched. When the sun rose, Ghost crawled out from under a pine tree into a forest that looked as if it were made of glass; every needle, every twig, and stem coated with a silvery sheath of ice.

The faithful, old dog walked on through the ice's cruel beauty, traveling east to an orchestra of falling drops as the day warmed and the ice thawed.

In spite of his pinched belly, Ghost kept clear of villages. People were dangerous and could not be trusted. All he was--all he had, was focused on one goal: getting back to Tarak.

E.F.WINTERS

He knew when he was getting close to the village but smells had changed, offering no comfort. Decay, disease, death greeted him.

Ghost whined and pushed himself to a trot.

With bruised and scabbed footpads, the old dog picked his path gingerly along the river's edge. Once, he stopped, perking up his ears, thinking he heard Tarak's voice on the wind, but it had stopped, and he could not be sure. He knew he was getting close though, and he knew that meant he had to be careful. The villagers here had not been kind to him. Ghost crept along the edge of the village's beach, lurking in the brush.

Overturned canoes were lined up above the high water mark; long straight furrows showing where they had been dragged across the beach. There were fresh footprints and the smell of bodies; dead and alive. People had been here not long ago. They were gone now--all but one. A large woman with long, dark, braids sat on her knees in the wet sand, gazing out at the water. Tears trickled down her cheeks as her fingers absently stroked a feather.

Ghost stared at the feather. He could smell Tarak on it--the scent of the boy's hair still tangled up in the sinew ties. A flood of memories swept over him; Tarak's hands stroking his back, the boy's arms wrapped around his neck, sleeping together in a tumble of boy and dog, running, swimming, hunting. Loneliness stabbed the old dog's heart and he puled softly.

CHAPTER 32

The woman turned and saw him, staring in disbelief.

"Ghost?" She whispered. "Are you Ghost?" She struggled to her feet.

Ghost spun and disappeared into the brush. The woman did not chase him, or throw anything. She sank back to her knees, looking down at the feather in her hands, not moving, but Ghost sensed her excitement in her quickened breath and racing heart. She acted like he was not there, but she knew he was.

Softly, she began to hum a working song sung by village women beneath Wai-i-ka. The notes sang to the old dog of memories; home, safety, and people who had loved him. "I am not a stranger," it said to him. "I know your people, and they are my people."

Before he knew it, Ghost was at the woman's side.

She did not try to touch him. She did not even look at him. Ghost sniffed the feather and whimpered.

"Yes, it's Tarak's. You smell him on it, don't you, old boy?" Big Woman studied the dog's scabbed face, his scarred side, thinning coat and sunken belly. "It was all true, wasn't it? Everything Tarak said. You were there on the bluff that day at Silaylo, and it was you who drew the bear away and saved them." She shook her head. "Tarak's imaginary white dog is not imaginary; he's real."

E.F. WINTERS

Ghost looked up and down the beach, searching for the boy that went with the feather.

"He's not here, Ghost. I'm sorry." Big Woman wiped tears from her cheeks. "But he's gone. He tried to wait for you but he couldn't. They took him, you see. They took him to Memeloose--to the island of the dead. He's there." She pointed across the water to a dark, shadowy hump in the distance. Ghost's black button eyes followed.

Pulling the sadness from the bottom of his soul, he stretched his nose to the sky and gave a long, mournful howl.

A twist of wind whipped the feather from Big Woman's hand, sending it spinning through the air. Springing to her feet, she chased it as it danced and twirled just out of reach.

Ghost jumped into the air, snapping at the feather with his teeth. It hovered over him then shot out over the water, falling on to the river's surface. He plunged in after it.

"No, Ghost!" Big Woman cried out.

The white dog was almost within reach of his prize when the wind again lifted the feather and sent it flying toward Memeloose. Paddling on through the frigid water, he followed.

Big Woman watched until all she could see was a white dot moving through the water in the distance.

"Look after them, Spirits." With heavy limbs, she climbed up the bank, turning to look

CHAPTER 32

back one last time. On the West wind came the distant song of voyageurs making their way upriver.

*****

Hefting their burden onto the rocky shore, the men from Gulasquo carried Tuck-na-wit's burial pallet to the House of the Dead.

Ten feet wide, fifteen feet long and dug six feet down into the earth, only a foot of the walls and the roof showed above the ground. There was no door. A low hole in the West wall was the only way in or out. When the villagers needed to get in, the opening was dug out. Then once their gruesome burdens had been deposited, the hole was filled back in.

The village men removed the rocks and dirt and waited for the bad air to clear before picking up the pallet and taking it inside.

Long, wooden shelves lined three walls, each heavy with the bodies of the dead. In the center of the room ran a bank of tables wide enough to hold burial pallets but so many tillikum had died, there was no place left for more. Older skeletons had been swept onto the floor to make space for newly dead and there they lay dressed in their rotting best, half wrapped in blankets, old and new; a puzzle of overlapping bones piled into corners. The old ways were crumbling under the weight of the epidemic.

The village men cleared a place for Tuck-na-wit on a shelf in the center of the room, set the pallet down, and began to shuffle out.

"He should be dead," one man muttered.

"He will be soon enough," another answered. "Don't worry, Chet'woot will not travel the star path alone."

Rocks scraped and clunked together as the men closed the opening back up.

Inside the burial lodge, it grew darker and darker, the men's voices growing muffled and faint, until finally there was no sound and no light at all. No matter how wide he opened his eyes, Tarak could not see anything, but he knew Tuck-na-wit's dead eyeballs stared back into his. He felt the weight of the dead lining the shelves and scattered across the floor. Memeloose was a place of death and it clawed at the living boy's mind.

"You are one of us now," spirit's whispered in scratches of bone on bone.

"No." The blood in Tarak's eardrums pounded, filling his head with the sound of his own heartbeat. He strained against the sinew that bound his wrists, ignoring the pain and the sticky warm liquid oozing around them. His blood smelled like the white man's metal. Tarak shifted. Something sharp pricked his chest.

Tuck-na-wit's bear claw, he thought. It was only a few inches from his face. Scrunching down on the pallet, Tarak stretched his neck out until he found the necklace with his lips. Careful not to cut

CHAPTER 32

himself on the sharp edge, he bit down. Holding the claw between his teeth, Tarak began moving his legs up and down, by tiny fractions of an inch, patiently working until the lower rope hung limp around his ankles like a deflated hoop. One at a time, he bent his numb legs and removed them from the ropes' circle. With his head on Tuck's cold chest, he rested for a moment, trying to catch his breath then emptying his lungs, he made himself as small as possible and began wriggling his body down toward the foot of the pallet. The last rope that bound him to Tuck-na-wit edged up. He hunched his shoulders together, squirmed out from under it and rolled away from his dead friend with a sob of relief. Falling to the floor, his head struck the ground and he blacked out.

When Tarak woke, his wrists throbbed and the sharp tang of his own blood was on his lips.

I am alive, he thought, with more than a little surprise, peering into the false twilight of the burial lodge and finding its darkness less complete than it had seemed before. Eyeless sockets leered at him. Bony hands beckoned.

"You are not free yet," the dead whispered, their toothless grins mocking the only living heartbeat among them.

"No, but I am not dead yet, either," Tarak answered back, stubbornly.

Then he heard it. The scratch, scratch, scratching of something, or someone, outside the house of the dead. The darkness around him rippled and everything slowed.

This is it, he realized. *This is my vision; the blackness, the bones, the scratching. I am walking inside the vision I was given so many moons ago on Wai-i-ka.*

Thin layers of skin grew over the skeletons in the corner until they became his friends who had been taken captive by the Snake; Chiwa-chni, Big Woman, Ti'caw, Yumis, and all the others.

The doe appeared among them, transforming from a deer into a woman with soft, dark eyes, and warm, brown skin. From the basket she carried she took small pieces of meat, giving a portion to each of the captives.

"Take what you need to live," she said. "I give it freely." But with each offering she gave, the doe-woman herself faded, becoming more translucent until, when the basket was empty, it fell to the ground.

Tarak looked at the captives, now renewed and hopeful. He had thought things had gone wrong that day when the Snake had taken his deer. He had told himself that he had been cheated. But he saw now, in this moment, that everything had gone as it was supposed to. The doe had given her life to him, not for him to take meat back to a village with plenty, but to feed the hungry captives so they could live.

"Thank you, sister," Tarak whispered to the deer's spirit. "Forgive this foolish person. I did

CHAPTER 32

not understand. I will try to be worthy of your gift."

"To do that, you must live," the doe-woman's voice replied.

Tarak's hand touched the sharp curve of Tuck-na-wit's bear claw lying behind him on the floor where it had dropped when he fell. He grasped it in his hand, bent his wrist back as far as he could and began sawing at the sinew that bound his wrists. As the last strand fell away, a slash of daylight, like a bright spear, burst into the darkness. Tarak squinted, blinking into the light.

Dusty sunbeams made a halo around the outline of a huge dog standing in the center of the lodge's doorway; its ears perched on top of its head like teepees.

"Ghost!" Tarak threw himself at his friend. "You came." Wrapping his arms around the dog's neck, he buried his face in Ghost's fur. "You found me." The dog laid his head on the boy's shoulder. Pressed together, their hearts beat as one.

Tarak sat back. The front of his tunic was soaked. "You swam?" He scratched the dog's ears. "Lemolo old bear." Tarak's hands sought out the scars and scabs that spoke of the adventures his friend had gone through--adventures he would never know about, except by the marks they had left. Ghost's coat felt dry and brittle beneath his hands and the skin between his ribs was sunken, but all that could be fixed, Tarak told himself. They were together. A warm, wet tongue scratched his cheek.

"I love you too, Old Bear."

Ghost raised his head, his ears pricked up; listening.

"Someone is coming. We need to go." Tarak stood unsteadily, rummaging on the pallet for Tuck-na-wit's broken knife. "I am sorry, Tuck," he apologized. "I cannot make this journey with you now, but we will see each other again in the spirit land and when we do, we will go hunting among the stars, you and I, and Ghost."

Using the knife, Tarak slashed a strip from his friend's buckskin shirt, wrapped it around his right wrist and tied it off with his teeth and left hand then did the same with the left hand to bind the left wrist. It was all he could do to slow the flow of blood from the wounds the sinew had made as they cut into his wrists. Picking up the bear claw, Tarak slipped it into the pouch Lala had made him.

"Come, Ghost." Tarak dropped to all fours and crawled out of The House of the Dead.

CHAPTER THIRTY-THREE

Low, gray clouds threatened more snow, making everything on the island seem close and small. Ghost looked south and huffed, his breath puffing bursts of steam into the cold air. The dry winter grass rustled.

Someone was coming through the meadow.

Tarak crouched behind the tall grass and pulled the dog up close beside him.

"Shush. Quiet now, Old Bear." He put his hands around Ghost's muzzle. Slowing his own breath, Tarak fixed his eyes on Ghost's, silently begging him to be still.

"You have nothing to fear, dear ones." The Bone Turner muttered to his invisible charges, his feet crunching through the crust of the day old snow. "I watched the village men close the opening myself. I would not let animals steal your bones."

The old man limped by, passing so close that Tarak could smell the stink of his clothes. As soon as he had passed, Tarak released Ghost's nose.

"Come on. We have to keep moving." Keeping a steadying hand on the dog's broad back, Tarak headed south toward the fringe of trees that outlined the edge of the island.

A wail rose behind them.

"He is gone! The slave boy is gone!" The Bone Turner screeched. "Oh, the spirit of Chet'woot will be angry. I must get him back. Don't worry, chief's son, I will find him. You will not travel to the spirit world alone. When someone is buried, they should stay buried!"

"Hurry, Ghost." Tarak forced himself to a ragged trot.

"Stop, slave! There is nowhere for you to go!" Slowed by age and the twisting of his deformed leg, the Bone Turner did not move quickly, but he did not have to. Tarak stumbled and faltered, his head spinning from the loss of blood. He caught himself on Ghost's back and ran. The bandages around his wrists soon soaked through, leaving smears of red on Ghost's white coat.

"West," Tarak panted. "We need to head west now," he struggled on.

"This time, I will poke a hole in you myself, slave boy," the Bone Turner's raspy voice threatened. "When the blood spills from your body, you will learn to stay put. Where do you think you are going anyway?" The man's words echoed back and forth across the gorge. "You have been buried. You cannot leave Memeloose. You are already dead...dead...dead!"

Fear tore at Tarak's resolve. What if they could not find a canoe that had not been "killed?" How would they get away from the island? Where could they go? Jimmy and Hyas Tee at Fort

CHAPTER 33

Vancouver seemed very far away. Tarak's vision blurred. Weaving his fingers more tightly into his friend's fur he let the dog lead pulling him on.

"You cannot run from me." The Bone Turner's shouts pushed them from behind. "There is nowhere for you to go. Do you hear me? You have seen the faces of the dead. You have heard their voices--you hear them now. You have no place in the world of the living."

Spectral wisps wove through the branches of the winter-thin trees and hollow-cheeked faces glowered at Tarak from the shadows. His insides shrank away from their cruel gazes and he held tightly to Ghost.

"I am not dead. I am not dead," he told himself over and over again.

"Boof." Ghost's wet nose on Tarak's cheek pulled him back to the physical world. Heavy clouds had shut out the last patch of blue and the wind's icy fingers fidgeted at the frayed edges of Tarak's tunic. Ghost had gotten them to the beach.

A cold rain began to fall.

To the West the main landing area connected to smaller beaches separated by spindly stands of young cottonwoods.

"Where? Where would it be?" Tarak scanned the shoreline for the working canoe the Bone Turner must have hidden somewhere.

A feather was lying on the wet sand, its edges fluttering in the wind.

E.F.WINTERS

Kamiakin's feather. Drawn forward, Tarak picked up the feather and held it, remembering the day the Kikiya leader had given it to him.

Kamiakin had said that a man could not belong to someone else; only to himself. Tarak did not belong to Tuck-na-wit, or Siniuse, and he certainly did not belong to the dead. He took one more, long look, searching the beach. There was no canoe, and no place left to go...except the river. The sky threatened snow and the water before them rippled, cold and deadly.

Tarak knelt beside Ghost, put his arms around the big dog's ruffed neck and pulled him close.

"I'm sorry, boy, there's no other way. We have to go into the river." Ghost looked at the freezing, gray water and whined. "I know you are tired and cold but you are also brave and strong hearted. We did it every day back home. A'cmu said it was what made us strong. Now we will prove to them just how strong we are."

Tarak stood and ran down the beach, splashing into the icy river, Ghost at his side.

The shock of the cold stole the breath from Tarak's body. Water raced to fill the spaces air had abandoned and Tarak sucked it into his lungs. But he could not breathe water.

"Please, Great River, please let us keep our lives," he pleaded with the river's spirit.

"Again you ask for favors, mountain boy? What will you give me in return?"

CHAPTER 33

"I have nothing," Tarak despaired. What would a river spirit want from a boy whose only thing of value was the love of a dog? *"No not that,"* he thought, quickly. *"Not Ghost. Take whatever you want from me but spare Ghost."* The spirit of the river was silent and Tarak felt himself sinking down through the water.

"There is something else you carry of value, something that is not yours," it bubbled.

Tarak could not think what the spirit meant.

"I will take it as an offering from the great heart to whom it rightfully belongs, but I cannot give him more life than is his," the river said, mysteriously. *"I can only give him time."*

The string on Tarak's pouch loosened and its mouth blossomed open. The bear claw Tuck-na-wit had claimed as proof of his victory, but which rightfully belonged to Ghost, floated out into the murky depths.

Tarak's head broke the surface and he sucked in freezing air, spluttering and coughing. Not far away, Ghost had found a log that had drifted into the island's backwater, and was swimming toward it. Tarak swam to it, holding the log steady and pushing Ghost's soggy rump onto it before dragging himself out.

Boy and dog lay shivering beside each other as the log slowly drifted into the main current, headed downriver.

E.F. WINTERS

"Stop, slave!" the Bone Turner shouted behind them. "You have been buried. You cannot leave. You are already dead!"

Icy rain turned to gentle snow and Tarak watched the flakes as they floated out of the sky. He could still feel Ghost's heart beating--not the strong, solid beat that had always anchored his life, but a thin, fragile knock that punctuated the white dog's rattling breath. Tarak wrapped his arms around the wet dog and held him close, trying to will what was left of his own warmth into Ghost's old bones.

"At least we are free and we will travel the Star Path together," Tarak whispered.

The faint thread of voices drifted from some unseen world across the water; sounds of the living wrapped in fog and dream.

Ghost's ears pricked up and he raised his head to listen.

They came again.

Leaping to his feet, and almost spilling them both back into the water, the white dog barked with his whole body from head to tail.

"It's coming from over there." The words were in the wawa of the King Georgemen and the Boston Kloochman; not Chinook. These were not villagers from Gulasquo come to return him to the House of the Dead.

Ghost barked with greater urgency.

The prow of a le boat parted the falling snow and Reverend Perkins, Winslow, Angus

CHAPTER 33

McDonald, Jimmy and Loo-ee peered out from behind it.

"It's him!" Jimmy shouted. "He's alive and he's off the island!"

"Smart lad, that one!" The men slapped each other on the backs as if they were responsible for Tarak's intelligence.

"Good boy, Ghost," Jimmy called out. "Hold on, we're coming, Tarak."

A cloud fogged the edges of Tarak's vision. He didn't feel cold. He didn't feel anything anymore. He just wanted to be left alone, to hold Ghost and sleep.

"Shush, Ghost. Quiet," he muttered, trying to pull the dog back down with him. Ghost stood over the boy like a protective mama bear.

"Hold steady, mon amis'," Loo-ee ordered.

"We've got him." Tarak felt himself lifted into the air.

"He must be half frozen to death," a woman's voice spoke up. "Here, wrap him in this." A blanket appeared. "Now give him to me," the woman inisted. "Oh, Henry, look at his wrists," she whispered, as Tarak was settled in her lap.

He opened his eyes. "Stay away! Get back!" Tarak struggled against the shadows crowded around him. "I am not dead! I am not dead! Ghost! Ghost! Where are you, Ghost?" He screamed.

A mass of white fur flew through the air, landing in the boat with a thud, and rocking it violently. Tarak's rescuers grabbed for anything to steady themselves as Ghost belly-crawled into his boy's lap.

"Well, that's one way to get the beastie on board," Angus announced, with a hearty laugh.

A lantern's flare pushed back the blue-gray world of death. Jimmy Buckeye's face hovered over Tarak.

"You got him, Mrs. Perkins?"

The mission woman Tarak had seen on the beach at Silaylo held him in a blanket. Angus McDonald, The Klale man, Winslow, Reverend Perkins, and Loo-ee bunched up behind him as Jimmy began to rub Ghost down and wrap him up as well.

"Settle down, cheechako. You're okay now. When Doc Gairdner came back without you, me and Loo-ee went straight to Hyas Tee," Jimmy explained. The Reverend and his missus heard and insisted we come upriver to buy you back, but when we got to Gulasquo, that old devil, Siniuse, told us you were already dead. We were just pushing off when a big woman came running down the beach waving her hands and shouting that you'd been buried alive on Memeloose. We were coming to dig you out when we heard this old kamooks here barking." Jimmy scratched Ghost's ear.

"It is all right now, son," the mission woman whispered, stroking Tarak's wet hair.

CHAPTER 33

"They can't hurt you anymore. You are safe. You are alive and free."

Alive and free. "Kloshe," Tarak whispered, laying his head on Ghost. They were alive and free and together again at last.

CHAPTER THIRTY-FOUR

Winter winds stormed through the gorge, leaving only the sturdy evergreens untouched by their freezing breath. The inhabitants of Wascopum Mission clutched heavy coats or blankets and tried to stay warm within their stockade walls. Forced to stay close to their fires, their world shrunk to four walls. Isolated by the bad weather, come February, settlers along the gorge could no longer escape the fact that winter's sharp blade was at their throats, wondering if they would make it to spring. "Cabin fever," the old timers called it telling tales of hapless loners going winter crazy.

But for Tarak, the world had become bigger than ever. Curled up with Ghost by the woodstove in the mission schoolhouse, he devoured the mysteries of the magic tzum-tzum lines, exploring places he had never imagined. Opening a book was like stepping into a canoe that could take you anywhere.

Tarak read stories about a boy named David, who bested a giant using only a slingshot. And another boy, whose brothers tried to kill him but who lived on to lead a great nation.

Under Elvira Perkins' care, the wounds on Tarak's wrists were healing but his dreams were

CHAPTER 34

haunted nightmares of being buried with hes friend on Memeloose.

Often, in the midst of reading, he would set the book aside, letting his mind drift South to Wai-i-ka. Then he would stroke Ghost's fur. "Soon, Old Bear, soon," he promised his friend, softly, absently, touching the feather he once again wore secretly beneath his shirt.

Mrs. Perkins had taken his old leather tunic, the cuffs stained with blood, and replaced it with a white man's store-bought shirt with chil-chil buttons running down the front. The missionaries had cut his hair, put hard-soled boots on his feet and named him Ransom. He had not objected. He had been called by many names, it did not change who he was. The relics of his past meant nothing to him, except Kamiakin's feather, and Ghost. Still, he often thought of Tuck-na-wit, wishing he could share all the strange things he was learning.

He hoped Big Woman was well and that Tot and his family had been spared from the fever. Though he watched canoes go up and down the river every day, he was not allowed to send word to his friends in Gulasquo. The slave boy, Tuck-na-wit's Friend, had been buried on Memeloose and he needed to stay there.

A loud rap on the schoolhouse door brought Tarak, Ghost, and Reverend Perkins' heads up. The door squeaked open on frozen hinges and Winslow ushered two bundled figures in.

"We have visitors from the Fort, Brother Perkins," he announced.

"Ko-ko! Kloshe Konaway." The smells of smoke, sweat, and animal skins gusted in as Loo-ee and Jimmy, their cheeks and noses apple-red, their fur coats stiff with ice, clomped inside, leaving slushy tracks of snow on the floor behind them. "Bon Jour, mon amis!" The Frenchman ruffled Tarak's hair fondly while Jimmy greeted Ghost. "Kahta Maika?"

"We are well, Brother Barbo. You'll stay for dinner, of course," Perkins offered.

Loo-ee's chapped hands hovered over the stove's warmth.

"Eef eet eez not too much trouble. Merci, Reverend. We thought we would check up on our leetle friend here and zee if he wants to come travel with us, eh?" The fur trapper wiped the melting ice from his mustache with the back of his hand, smoothing the fur that covered his face and winked at Tarak.

Reverend Perkins, placed a marker in his book and closed it, his brows knit. "People say it will be cold yet for at least another month or two."

"A good time for trapping. Pelts are full and thick," Loo-ee assured him.

"Boston men pay big dolla for winter furs." Jimmy grinned at Tarak.

Perkins turned to Tarak. "Tarak, would you let Mrs. Perkins know that we will have company for dinner?"

CHAPTER 34

"Yes, Brother Perkins." Tarak pulled his blanket around his shoulders and walked slowly to the door. Ghost unwound himself with a sigh and joined him.

"You want the boy to trap beaver, Messieur Barbo?"

"He eez old enough, and eet weell not hurt him to learn a trade. Zee trapping eez a good, honest living."

"Let's be honest, Gentleman. There are few beaver left. They have been trapped out. The time of the fur trapper is ending. Tarak is a good boy with a quick mind. He has a thirst for knowledge. He deserves better."

"And you think you can give him that?" Jimmy demanded, defensively.

Loo-ee silenced him with a glance. "Excuse moi, Reverend, but downriver, we hear you have troubles at zee mission. Some leetle ones they have been getting sick, no?" The young missionary hung his head. "I know zeese is not what you intended. You are a good man, but zee mission school has become a death sentence for zee tenas tillikum who stay here." He looked at Tarak.

Perkin's eyes mirrored the deep pain of his spirit. It was a hard truth but one he could not deny. As the recent swarm of settlers had spread across the territory, disease had followed. The good that he and his wife had come to bring to the tillikum had backfired. The school had become a place to learn about death and each night more of the children who boarded, there stole away to return to their homes. It was no use telling them they were probably taking the sickness with them. They were afraid, and they wanted to go home.

Even adult tillikum had begun to stay away, leaving only a few faithful followers to do the work.

A gust of cold entered with Elvira Perkins, Tarak and Ghost trailing close behind her.

Tarak had watched as Mrs. Perkin's kind, blue eyes had taken on the same sad look that had haunted Naha's, her white hands fluttering like fragile birds, wanting to caress the Native children she loved, yet afraid to touch.

Even the dignified creases of old Winslow's face had become deeper and more careworn this long winter.

"We were thinking maybe Tarak should come back with us now that he's feeling better," Jimmy suggested.

Winslow and Elvira both looked to the young Reverend. Tarak had become more than just another student. He was a prodigy, symbolizing the success they had hoped for.

"You must know zat zees eez not his place," Loo-ee said, quietly, reading their faces.

"It could be," Perkins argued, hoarsely.

"With all zeese settlers comes more sickness and more death. He has seen enough of eet. Let him go."

CHAPTER 34

Winslow stepped forward, wearing the dignity of his age and character like a suit of armor.

"You always say there are no slaves here, Reverend, that we are all equal in the sight of our Creator. The boy is a free man. There is no reason to even have this conversation. This is Tarak's decision.

Mrs. Perkins floated to her husband's side, looping her arm through his.

"Winslow's right, Henry." She squeezed her husband's arm. "Keeping Ransom in our world is selfish. His parents don't even know if he is dead or alive. How would we feel if it was our son? If this is not the life the boy wants, it would be just another kind of slavery."

"But he is so bright, Elvira. He's learned so much. He could be a bridge between our peoples, all that we hoped for and worked for." Reverend Perkins' eyes met his wife's. Once, they had believed in what they were doing, but the deaths of the mission children were eating away at that certainty.

"It was our dream, Henry, not Ransom's."

Reverend Perkins nodded. "They are right, Ransom. You are your own man. This is your decision, not ours."

Tarak looked down at Ghost. "We want to go home." All that stood in their way was miles and miles of mud and snow.

"When the snow melts," Loo ee announced.

"When the snow melts," Tarak repeated.

CHAPTER THIRTY-FIVE

"Hyas Tee said for you to choose out whatever you needed." Jimmy, Tarak and Ghost stepped lightly over the spongy, rain-soaked grass of the fort's open green, headed for the company store. The smoke of forges and the scent of freshly-baked bread mixed with the rhythmic clang of blacksmiths and the shouts of voyageurs calling from the waterfront. More trappers returned from the outer lands every day now, their packs loaded with rich, winter furs.

Spring had come to the Pacific Northwest, pushing the gloomy, low-hanging clouds on across the country. Pale spindles of new growth poked up through the dried bouquets of strawberry plants that lined the fort's pathways. A fresh new world sang with green beneath a sky that was blue at last.

"I don't need anything, Jimmy. Really." Tarak looked down at Ghost, who smiled back. The old dog had gained enough weight that the lines of his ribs did not show through his fur anymore but the scars on his nose and along his side remained bare.

Tarak had scars too. The skin over his wrists was red and puckered, but the deepest scars he bore were inside, where no one saw them.

CHAPTER 35

Jimmy's fingers plucked at the knees of Tarak's hand-me-down pants. Bony ankles showed below the hem. Jimmy laughed. It was a solid, friendly laugh, with no meanness in it.

"What is so funny, mon-ami?" Loo-ee joined them.

Jimmy pointed at Tarak's exposed ankles. "He says he does not need anything."

Loo-ee raised an eyebrow. "Cheechako, you look like a cricket in a ladybug's trousers. You need zee proper pants."

The Frenchman led Tarak and Ghost into the company store. Inside, it smelled like pine, wool, and the bitter drink that white men called 'coffee'. Men were leaning over the counter talking about what they'd seen and heard or stories they made up over the winter.

"Some folk are headin' to the Black Hills in the Dakotas. They're saying there's gold there for the taking."

"Indian country," his companion grunted. "You won't catch me going there."

"Well, what do you think this is, you simpleton? This is all Indian country."

The man frowned. "Not like there. Them Indians are the scalpin' kind. Ours here are just regular folk."

His friend shook his head. "I'd be more worried about those land-grabbin' gold miners than the Indians. Them fellows don't respect nothing comes between them and their money."

"Morning, Loo-ee... Jimmy." The shopkeeper looked at Tarak. "Is this the boy that everyone's talking about?"

Loo-ee clasped Tarak's shoulder. "Oui, and he eez a boy no longer, Messieur Gray, as you can zee. Heez britches no longer suit him."

The shop's shelves held neatly folded stacks of ready-made clothes, blankets and the calico material the Indians called tzum sill.

The shopkeeper picked through a stack of pants until he found a pair he judged would be a reasonable fit.

"What about these?" He held the dark trousers up to Tarak's waist. "They look to be of a size, with some room for growing." The pant legs puddled around Tarak's feet. Ghost sniffed the brushed wool. "You'll have to roll them up for a few months maybe, but young men your age grow fast."

"We weell take zem," Loo-ee announced. "Dr. McLoughlin says to put zem on the company account."

"Settlers, widows, orphans; Doctor McLoughlin's generosity knows no bounds." The shopkeeper turned to make an entry on his accounts.

"He eez a good man," Loo-ee agreed.

"He is a great man, but the Company don't take much to his helpin' ways, especially him helpin' out all these settlers."

"He cannot just let zem starve."

CHAPTER 35

The merchant shrugged. "He is a Christian man, no question, but the Company sent him here to look after the fur trade, not a bunch of Americans with an eye to taking over the territory."

"Well, I'd hate to see what would happen if they tried to put someone else in charge of this place," the man who had been talking about the gold rush in the Black Hills added.

"Zere would be war on zee river within a year,"Loo-ee predicted loyally. "A stranger cannot hold the tillikum togezer; only Hyas Tee has zee heart for zat. Zere eese a reason zee fort's cannon has never been fired, Messieur, and zat reason is Hyas Tee. The Company knows zeese."

"I hope you're right, Messieur Barbo," the shopkeeper replied.

"Give us three of zee sugar candies, too. I weell pay for them." Loo-ee winked at Tarak. "We must celebrate, mon amis."

The new pants covered Tarak's ankles, the extra material folded over several times making wide cuffs at the bottom.

"What are we celebrating, Loo-ee?" Tarak asked as they headed for the fort's gate, Ghost padding along beside them.

Loo-ee flourished his hand. "You're coming of age, of course. In my country, eet eez a big day when zee young messieur gets his first pair of zee long pants. Mamas cry, little brothers pout, and pretty girls wink at you." He winked, though he was neither pretty nor a girl. "Eet eez a sign to everyone zat you are a man now, no?"

Jimmy popped a candy into his mouth as they passed into Kanaka village.

Outside the fort walls, the needs of survival and the buzz of jargon glued the mismatched community of Europeans, Polynesians and indigenous locals together.

"Listen to zat. You hear? You do not have to travel zee world to get an education. Just come to Fort Vancouver and eet will come to you," Loo-ee bragged.

"Tarak!" The crowd parted and Big Woman sailed toward them, her huge body teetering on a pair of European style, lace-up boots. A calico print, "tzum sil" dress swung with the sway of her hips and a fine wool blanket was spread jauntily across her shoulders. Her solid arms swelled around Tarak's shoulders.

"I am so happy to see you alive, little brother."

"I am so happy to be alive, thanks to you." Tarak laughed. "Mahsie."

"And the big, white dog, too." Big Woman released Tarak and reached out to Ghost, who allowed himself to be petted. "This is my husband." She nodded at the silent, little man hidden behind her. Tarak recognized him as the Chinook who had been her master. "His wife died of the fever but I nursed him back to health, so now, I am his wife." The Chinook man looked at

CHAPTER 35

the female force of nature that was Big Woman with an expression of perplexed awe.

"You will not go home then?" Tarak asked.

"I may visit someday to show off my rich husband." Big Woman tossed her head. "But I have a new home now. So many in Gulasquo died of the sickness." She clicked her tongue. "The village is very different. My husband is one of the richest men there and with my help, he will take his place as a chief man among his people." Her dark eyes twinkled. "But you, when will you make the trip back to Wai-i-ka?"

Tarak hesitated, his eyes straying to the South as if he could see across the many miles separating him from his village. He looked down at Ghost. In the seven months since he had been taken from his home, Tarak had grown up but Ghost had grown old. The old dog had many aches and pains and he did not eat as easily as he used to. Tarak had hoped that the arrival of spring would return the bounce to his friend's step. It had not. But they could not wait much longer. "Soon I think. Soon." He stroked Ghost's fur.

"Come see me before you go. I have something for you." Big Woman hugged Tarak again, whispering, "I found your pack and the ashes. I hid it. You will take Ti'caw's ashes back home when you go, won't you?"

Tarak nodded, barely hearing her words. The blood had rushed to his head and his ears were buzzing. An old man was walking toward them.

"Siniuse..." The word came out a gasp. Tarak had almost not recognized the stern man who had bought him at Silaylo. Siniuse's dark, black hair was striped with gray, his arrow-straight back bent like the twisted junipers that grew on the gorge's windblown heights. In the emptiness left by Naha and Tuck-na-wit's deaths, the once proud leader had shrunk to half his former self. Tot walked at his brother-in-law's side, slowing as he saw Tarak and his friends. Quickly, he tried to steer Siniuse away.

Ghost growled.

Loo-ee, Jimmy and Big Woman moved to shield Tarak.

"No." Tarak stepped out from behind them. "I am a man. I must face this axe' ki myself."

Siniuse looked up, stumbling as the color drained from his face.

"Skookum!" he shrieked, raising a hand up to look at Tarak through his fingers. "Stay back!"

"Shh, brother. Don't make a scene," Tot tried to quiet the elder man. "There is no spirit there. You are seeing things. You are still not well."

People began to turn and stare at the old Chinook.

Ghost growled again.

"It's okay, Ghost," Tarak told him. Tarak had thought he hated this man who had bought his life and then thrown it away so easily, but all he felt now was pity.

CHAPTER 35

Siniuse lowered his hand. "You are not a skookum? You are alive?"

Tarak nodded. "Yes."

The old man's eyes hardened. "And my son is dead."

"My brother also," Tarak reminded him.

Tot took Siniuse's arm. "Come. We should go." Siniuse shook him off, his eyes squinting to slits.

"You belong to me, slave."

"No." Tarak shook his head slowly. "I belong to no one. Your son freed me before he died."

"You are a liar."

Tarak took a deep breath. "No, I am a free man. The slave you buried with your son is gone. The man before you is a different person. He has no master in this world."

The fire in Siniuse's eyes flickered and faded. "You are mine," he said again without conviction. "Chako. Come with me. There is no one in my lodge now." His voice became a whimper. "No wife, no sons...." His pleas hung in the air like wet laundry, stretched out and limp.

Tarak shook his head. "I am sorry, uncle. Whatever path remains for you, you must walk it alone. My life is not yours to take." Tarak turned and walked away. If his knees shook, no one could see it in his new long pants.

CHAPTER THIRTY-SIX

It was the moon of "Tat Hellum;" the time for fishing for sucker-fish when Tarak and Ghost began their journey back to Wai-i-ka. Loo-ee would not go with them. He was courting a woman and there were no beaver on the Upper Klamath, but Jimmy came along, saying he wished to visit his mother's people.

After a few days, Tarak and Jimmy could see that the long days of traveling were too much for their old friend and they slowed their pace, shortening the hours they traveled and taking long rests at midday. They waited patiently, visiting through his afternoon naps, and encouraging him to stop and play in the shallows of creeks and rivers, because they knew how much it pleased him. But halfway through the trip, even this slow pace became too much. They built a travois and took turns pulling Ghost along the trail.

"He rides like the King Georgeman," they laughed, avoiding the truth of their silent worries. The brave dog's spirit was as strong as ever but his body was failing.

On the banks of the river that white men called the Rogue, the two friends parted, vowing to visit each other soon.

CHAPTER 36

"You will be all right by yourself?" Jimmy asked, glancing at Ghost on the travois.

"I will not be by myself. Ghost will be with me."

"I could go with you, if you want?"

"We're fine." Tarak assured him.

Jimmy knelt by Ghost's side, his hands stroking the dog's warm fur. "It has been an honor traveling with you, Old Bear," he said softly. "I am a better person because I have known you. You have shown me how to be a true and loyal friend." Ghost's dark eyes smiled gently up into Jimmy's. "Safe journey, you will not be forgotten, Great Heart."

Jimmy looked back at them once and then was gone.

Once again, the world shrunk down to just the two of them; Ghost and Tarak.

Tarak gave Ghost water from his gourd and chewed bits of jerky until they were soft before slipping them between the dog's teeth, trying to keep his friend's strength up. They sat by the fire together in the evenings and slept curled around each other at night. Lulled by the sound of their two heartbeats, Tarak's nightmares faded then disappeared.

Tarak pulled the travois through the rocky gorges and up the dusty paths until one morning he looked up and Wai-i-ka towered over them, its white cap holding up the blue sky.

"Look, Ghost; the mountain. We're almost home." Tarak's spirit soared.

Lupine and tiny, white, alpine flowers blanketed the floor of the high meadows, welcoming the travelers. Old songs that Tarak thought he had forgotten seemed to rise up out of the ground and he sang them as he pulled the travois on.

"It won't be long now," Tarak assured his friend, his excitement building. Who would he see when he got there? Would they know him right away? How could they when he had changed so much?

Ghost raised his head and looked around as if he knew just where they were, his ears sitting up straight on his white head, his black lips curling up in a doggy smile.

Even the trees and rock formations along the trail began to look familiar, the scent of pine and summer grass swirling with memories. Tarak could count the turns now until he would see the rooftops of his village.

Ghost's breathing was shallow but his eyes winked in the dappled sunlight, watching the branches of the trees pass overhead.

Tarak pulled the travois around a bend and looked up. A doe stood in the path, its side turned toward him, its heart beating just beneath the ribs. Slowly, he slipped the bow from his shoulder, knocked an arrow, and aimed.

CHAPTER 36

Sunlight played across the doe's tan coat. A breeze fluttered the feather in Tarak's hair.

The doe raised her head and looked into the young hunter's eyes.

He had been kidnapped, sold into slavery, fought a bear, and been buried on Memeloose. No one had given him a ceremony, or a new name, but whether or not he took this deer's life now, he was a man. Tarak lowered his bow.

"Go home, little sister," he said softly. "Our families wait for us. A man takes only what he needs, and I do not need to celebrate my homecoming by stealing yours. Let us both go home tonight." The doe bounded away.

Somewhere in the distance, a Coyote howled.

Tarak smiled as he put away his bow and arrow and turned to lift the travois poles.

Ghost was sitting up tall and strong, just looking at him and smiling his black-lipped, doggy smile.

"Well, look at you. Feeling better?" Tarak knelt and ran his hands through the dog's white fur. It smelled like warm sunshine, pine, and sage. Ghost leaned his body into Tarak's, laying his head on Tarak's shoulder.

"I love you too, Old Bear." Tarak chuckled. He held the dog so close there was no space between them. "No one has ever had a greater heart or been a truer friend."

Sighing, Ghost lay back down onto the travois, his strength slipping away as mysteriously as it had come. Tarak felt a sudden tightening in his belly.

"No. Don't go, Ghost, not now," he begged, choking the words out past the knot of emotion in his throat. "Hold on. It's only a little bit further. We're almost there." He rose quickly, picking up the poles. "Mother and Iri'wa will know what to do to heal you. They'll have you up and around in no time." He wanted to believe it. He had never wanted to believe anything so badly in his life.

"Spirit, please, please..." his heart formed the prayer that his tongue could not.

At the top of the hill, the smell of acorn soup and wood smoke came curling through the treetops. Tarak looked down toward his family's lodge and in spite of his concern for his friend, his heart leapt. His mother and little sisters were there by the fire, laughing as they dropped acorns into a cook basket. *They are alive*, he thought joyously.

"We've made it, Ghost and they are alive!"

Behind him on the travois, Ghost let out a long, slow breath and sank back into a stillness where pain could not follow.

From the mouth of her cave, Iri'wa looked up.

A young man stood at the trailhead. Her eyes crinkled into a smile as the spirit of a large, white dog stepped up beside him.

CHAPTER 36

"So, you have returned him to us after all, Great Heart. You went in search of a boy and brought us back a man."

Ata' stepped out of the lodge and looked up at the trailhead. There at the top of the hill, stood his son. With a cry of joy, he began running up the path toward Tarak.

"You will not be forgotten, Ghost; Great Heart," Iri'wa promised Ghost's spirit. "We will tell your story for many years; the story of a dog and his boy." Tears ran down her face as Tarak flew down the path and into his father's arms. He and Ghost had come home.

*****

EPILOGUE

Tarak

What became of Tarak (not his real name) whom the Perkins' had re-named Ransom (historically correct), is not historically certain. According to one pioneer account, after being rescued from Memeloose, he went on to Jason Lee College in Salem, Oregon, where he became a minister and a teacher before returning to lead his people. This account, however, infers that he returned to the Yakima people and experts at the Strong Heart Library on the Yakima Reservation say that the pioneer account is in error. In other accounts, Tarak's fate is not mentioned beyond his rescue and we are left to imagine what happened. In 1848 however, gold was discovered at Sutters Mill near the location of Tarak's winter village. The arrival of gold miners in the region was a disaster for Native people who saw their population decimated by disease and genocide within a decade. In my heart, I hope the young man I have called Tarak, was able to return to his people to help them through this terrible time.

SOURCES

Ghost

The real Ghost came to live with our family, appearing in the mountains of Southern California alone and battered, with sore paws and deep scratches on his nose. Insisting he was going home with us, he remained by my side for many years, a loyal friend and companion, with a heart as big as the world. I promised him as he was dying that he would not be forgotten. I have now kept that promise. It was an honor.

Hyas Tee

In 1846, Doctor John McLoughlin, known along the Great River (the Columbia) as "Hyas Tee", the "Silver Haired Eagle", retired with his wife, Marguerite, from The Hudson's Bay Company to his property at the Willamette Falls (Oregon City). During his time as Chief Factor, people along the river were proud to say that the great cannons at Fort Vancouver were never fired. In 1957, he was posthumously named "The Father of Oregon."

The Perkins

The Reverend Henry Perkins and his wife, Elvira, left the Wascopum mission in 1844 after a disagreement with administrators back east, who did not understand the challenges of running a mission in the multi-cultural Pacific Northwest. He and Elvira had spent much of their time learning and documenting local languages in the belief that they should preach sermons and witness to their "parish" in their native tongues.

Kamiakin

After being a voice for peace and co-operation with whites for many years, Kamiakin, a well respected leader among the Yakima and other tribes, joined his voice to those calling the First Nations to fight against efforts to take their land. The battles became known as the Yakima Indian Wars of 1855. Kamiakin himself survived, escaping to Canada, where he lived until his return in 1860. He died sometime in 1877, living out his days on his own land in spite of multiple efforts to remove him.

SOURCES

SOURCES FOR MEMELOOSE
The Island of the Dead:

Arnold, Mable. *In the Land of the Grasshopper Song.* Lincoln: Bison. 1980.

Boyd, Robert. People of the Dalles: The Indians of Wascopam Mission. Lincoln: University of Nebraska Press, 1996.

Brosnan, Cornelius J. *Jason Lee-Prophet of the New Oregon. New York:* MacMillan. 1932.

Curtis, Edward S. *North American Indian vol. 7,* Evanston: Northwestern University. 2003

Gorham, Michael. *The Real Book About Indians.* Garden City: Garden City Books, 1953.

Hunn, Eugene S., James Selam. *Nch'i-wana: the Big River mid-columbia Indians and Their Land.* Seattle: University of Washington Press. 1989

Warren, Ester. *The Columbia Gorge Story.* (self-published). 1977

Levin, James A, Clifton David. *Klamath personalities: ten Rorschach case studies.* Lawrence: Dept. of Sociology and Anthropology Univ. of Kansas. 1963.

McWhorter, Lucullus Virgil. *The Tragedy of the Wahk-Shum – The Death of Andrew J. Bolon, Indian Agent to the Yakima Nation in Mid-September, 1855.* Fairfield: Ye Balleon Press. 1968

Splawn, A.J. *Ka-mi-akin – Yakima Indians Last Hero of the Yakimas.* Caldwell: Caxton Printers Ltd. 1917.

Taylor, Colin. *Myths of the North American Indians.* Lyndhurst: Barnes and Noble Books. 1995.

Other Research and Interviews:

The Strong Heart Collection: Yakama Cultural Center, Toppenish, WA

The L.V. McWhorter Photo Collection

Pictoral Archives of the Oregon Historical Society
www.ohs.org

Klamath Indian Tribe, Wasco Indian tribe,
www.accessgenealogy.com
Native American Genealogy: Shasta Indian tribe, Athapascan Indian History (uncredited) (www.accessgenealogy.com)

SOURCES

Shasta Indians: Territory, Glover. Social Organization, Glover Worldview, Glover (www.siskiyous.edu)

Native American Folklore of Shasta: un-credited (www.siskiyous.edu)

Indian Names for Moons, Days and other Calendar Stuff Konstatin 1996
(www.americanindian.net)

Centennial History of Oregon, Gaston
(gesswhoto.com/centenntial-indian-population)

Rogue River Indians and relations with Whites
(www.id.mind.net)

Clackamas County Timeline
 (www.usgennet.org)

Winning the Oregon Country Fairs 1911 Missionary education movement of the U.S. and Canada

Unpublished manuscripts of Thomas Talbot Waterman – interviewed 1910-1920

Coyote and Rock and other Lushotseed Stories

E.F. WINTERS

Columbia Plateau Indian Tribes – Whitman Mission NHS History and Culture-National Park Service U.S. Dept. of the Interior

Crater Lake National Park: Klamath Indians (Ritual and Worldview) National Park Service (compiled from the works of Winthrop Associates Cultural Research

Early Washington Maps: A Digital Collection Washington State University Library

Columbia Gorge Discovery Center- WascoCounty Historical Museum, The Dalles, OR. Compiled from works of Winthrop Association Cultural Research

Columbia Gorge Interpretive Center and Museum Stevenson, WA. National Park Service

Jennifer Brown. Interviews and Guidance: Ridgefield National Wildlife Refuge: Manager

Virginia Parks. U.S. Fish and Wildlife Service, (Cultural Resources Team) Sherwood OR

The Dalles Lock and Dam (pamphlet and tour) U.S. Army Corp of Engineers Portland Dist.

SOURCES

Joy Werlink. Washington State Historical Society Research Center, (Manuscript Specialist) Tacoma Washington

This project began as an oral story that I told for many years in classrooms and special events in the Pacific Northwest and Southern Nevada. The basic facts were discovered during research in pioneer archives in Oregon. To those who asked me to write the story down so you could share it with your own families, I have now kept that promise. A second promise is fulfilled with the addition of Ghost. He, too, actually lived, but in this century not the one before last.

I've tried to be respectful. I've tried to be honest. Sometimes the facts eluded me; sometimes I made changes to fit the story. I apologize if I have offended either the living or the dead. My intention is to encourage the pride of a new generation and inspire readers to find their own good path and walk it with honor.

If you enjoyed this book, please consider reading one of my other offerings:

SHARKS AND MINNOWS: (Teen Fantasy) The first in a series about a tough teenage girl whose messy life is complicated by special "gifts" that put her in harm's way.

(Watch for) EBULON: book one in THE KEEPERS OF THE TRUTHS series; (Young Adult Science Fiction/Fantasy), a collision of technology and magic, in a post apocalyptic multiverse battling over resources.

SOURCES

E. F. Winters has worked as a storyteller, writer, and director in the Pacific Northwest, the East Coast and Southern Nevada, telling stories from campfires to classrooms to the prestigious Venetian Resort in Las Vegas. She has been a pioneer in using the arts to teach life skills to Talented and Gifted, as well as At Risk populations. She currently lives in the mountains of Southern Nevada.

Connect with me Online:
Facebook:http//facebook.com/efwinters

www.ingramcontent.com/pod-product-compliance
Lightning Source LLC
Chambersburg PA
CBHW020356080526
44584CB00014B/1049